CHRIST IN CHURCH LEADERSHIP

Discovery House Publishers

Books, music, and videos that feed the soul with the Word of God

Box 3566 Grand Rapids, MI 49501

CHRIST IN CHURCH LEADERSHIP

A Handbook for Elders and Pastors

by Paul Winslow
and Dorman Followwill

Christ in Church Leadership: A Handbook for Elders and Pastors
by Paul Winslow and Dorman Followwill
Copyright © 2001 by Paul Winslow and Dorman Followwill

Discovery House Publishers is affiliated with
RBC Ministries, Grand Rapids, Michigan 49512.

Discovery House books are distributed to the trade exclusively by
Barbour Publishing, Inc., Uhrichsville, Ohio 44683.

Cover design by DesignTeam, Grand Rapids, Michigan
Photo by Alan Abramowitz / Stone

Unless indicated otherwise, Scripture is taken from the
New American Standard Bible (NASB).
Copyright © 1960, 1977 by the Lockman Foundation.

Library of Congress Cataloging-in-Publication Data

Winslow, Paul, 1935–
    Christ in church leadership : a handbook for elders and pastors
/ by Paul Winslow & Dorman Followwill.
        p. cm.
    ISBN 1-57293-066-7
    1. Christian leadership. 2. Christian leadership--Biblical teaching. 3. Typology
(Theology) I. Followwill, Dorman, 1965– II. Title.

 BV652.1 .W52 2001
253—dc21

                                                                00-065662

Printed in the United States of America.

03 04 05 06 07 08 09 10 / CHG / 10 9 8 7 6 5 4 3 2

Contents

INTRODUCTION

This book is the result of a partnership between two men who have been graced by God to learn firsthand both biblical and experiential truth in the arena of the leadership and functioning of a local church. Both men are former businessmen who have been called and gifted by God to become pastors. One is older with three grown and married children. The other is younger with five children still at home. Both have wives who know the Scriptures and minister to many.

We would like to acknowledge our great debt to the leaders who have set the example before us: Ray Stedman, Ed Stirm Sr., Bob Smith, Dave Roper, Charlie Luce, Bob Roe, and the elders of Peninsula Bible Church and Valley Bible Church. These godly men led the way by word and by deed. We are truly grateful for both. We also want to thank our wives who have shared our journey and never failed to encourage and support us.

Our reason for writing this book is that we believe the Lord and Head of the Church has asked us to do so. It is our prayer that God will open the minds of each reader to hear and understand His truth, and that the pages of this book will act as stepping stones toward this end.

Your brothers in Christ,

Dorman Followwill, the younger
Paul Winslow, the older

FOREWORD

What Is Body Life?

Adapted from the book *Body Life,* by Ray Stedman

As the violent decade of the 1960s faded into history and the hopeful year of 1970 began, the Body Life service at Peninsula Bible Church in Palo Alto, California, was born. At a New Year's Eve service on December 31, 1969, the camaraderie and love among the people was so evident that the pastoral staff met the next week and asked, "Why can't we have meetings like this all the time? How can we keep this beautiful spirit of love and mutual ministry going in our church?"

Out of those questions grew a determination to hold a service where people could bear one another's burdens and confess their sins and pray for one another as the Scripture commanded. Sunday evenings became the regular time for this special experience they called the "Body Life service."

The Body Life service started slowly, but soon a climate of honest realism took hold. When word of this invigorating new experience got around, local youths began to appear without any particular invitation. Many of them were long-haired, barefoot, and in bizarre dress. The middle-class Christians who regularly attended PBC gulped at this new development, but they determined to be genuinely Christian. They welcomed the young people, listened to them, prayed with them, and opened their hearts. Not surprisingly, the youth responded in the same way.

Church attendance increased by leaps and bounds. Every service was different. Love, joy, and a sense of acceptance prevailed so strongly that awed visitors frequently remarked about a spiritual atmosphere they could almost scoop up in their hands.

More than three decades have passed since that joyous time. The Jesus Movement of the tie-dyed, flower-power '60s and '70s is gone. Many of the features that characterized Body Life at PBC have changed with the times. In fact, there are no more "Body Life" services.

But genuine Body Life continues! The vitality, the openness, the acceptance, the caring, and the forgiveness live on. So too do the principles that guided Peninsula Bible Church through a time of unprecedented growth and an outpouring of supernatural love.

Paul Winslow, one of the authors of *Christ in Church Leadership*, was privileged to be a part of those Body Life services. His coauthor, Dorman Followwill, eventually joined the staff at PBC. Together these two men have laid out the biblical principles that helped guide the Body Life concept.

On the pages of this book, the authors share with their readers the same New Testament ideal of servant-leadership that they have shared with churches across the country and around the world. It is an ideal embodied by the true Servant-Leader, our Lord Jesus Christ.

Christ in Church Leadership will show you the scriptural principles that God intended to shape church government. It will provide you with practical hands-on advice to help your church continue in a Holy Spirit-led direction. May the Lord be glorified and His church strengthened as you read this book!

PART I:

Elders: Definitions & Descriptions

Chapter One

The Lead Man

The man was walking on ahead—leading the way. He was a pilgrim whose journey had begun in the northern province of Galilee, where He was well known. He loved the hillsides and openness of the country plains and valleys. He delighted in the seashore and the fisher folk who lived there.

But Galilee lay behind. He had crossed over to the other side of the Jordan, to the east. Now traversing back to the west, He stood by the banks of the Dead Sea. There, at 1,312 feet below sea level, He gazed up from the lowest point on the face of the earth.

Slowly He began wending his way uphill toward Mount Zion, the mountain of God. The narrow path clung to the side of a rocky wadi, the bottom occasionally disappearing from sight. Stones, bleached white by the desert sun, dotted the landscape. Few plants could survive here. It was an inhospitable land, dusty and dry.

The heavily-robed man perspired as he patiently toiled uphill. Perhaps He saw in that journey a metaphor for His life.

He had been born to a pilgrim couple, in a cave at night, in a land oppressed under Rome's iron boot. His mother's pregnancy was scandalous. His father was a woodworker, without title or land holdings. His family name carried no clout. For thirty years He had lived in obscurity, working with wood, overseeing the family business, studying and memorizing the Hebrew Scriptures.

But in three short years, the combination of His penetrating words, powerful miracles, and voices from heaven that attested to His deity had catapulted Him to prominence. It had been an uphill climb, and He was now scaling the most difficult height yet. Ever upward, further up and further forward, step by step.

As He walked steadily uphill, He lifted his eyes. He was going to Jerusalem—to Calvary. He led the way, choosing the path, leading in prayer, knowing where the road was heading. He was a leader. He was *the* leader. He was the *only* leader.

He still is.

Leadership on its knees

Elder leadership is "servant leadership," and the concept of servant leadership brings Mark 10:35–45 to mind. That passage concludes with Jesus' stirring words:

> **Whoever wishes to be first among you shall be slave of all. For even the Son of Man did not come to be served, but to serve, and to give His life a ransom for many.**
>
> *Mark 10:44–45*

Prior to this conversation, Jesus had provided the perfect metaphor for elder leadership in His journey to Jerusalem. As He walked on ahead, Jesus led the disciples to Jerusalem so that He could die on a cross.

Now He leads His church to a new Jerusalem, full of His glory, so that we might all share in that glory.

That first journey back to Jerusalem was an uphill road. Today, biblically-based eldership in a local church is an uphill journey. It is leadership by prayer and careful listening, not bullet-points or bullying. It is leadership by consensus, not coercion. It is leadership in which no single man is to dominate, even though many men around the circle may have dominant personalities. It is leadership born out of brotherhood, not star quality or popularity. It is leadership that operates more slowly than the chain of command and, at times, seems hopelessly inefficient.

And, since the first job of the elders is to discern and lead in accord with the mind of Jesus Christ, it is leadership on its knees (1 Corinthians 2:16; John 15:15; 16:13–16; 17:6–8).

Who among us has a mental picture of a leader humbly on his knees? Most of us cannot identify with that image of leadership. Rather, we recall images such as the stirring portrait of George Washington crossing the Delaware. In that painting, we see the strain of emotion etched on the faces of the men. Our eyes are drawn in contrast to General Washington's unflappable confidence and serenity. Impervious to the cold, untouched by the fears of the common men around him, he seems illumined by some inner light of greatness. That is the majestic and exalted portrait of leadership our egos want to embrace.

Biblical eldership, however, is leadership on its knees. It is not about power, positions, or titles—it is all about Jesus Christ and what He wants. And He often leads us on a rocky, uphill path.

All of this is why Jesus' journey to Jerusalem in Mark 10 is the key to understanding elder leadership.

The story starts in Mark 10:32:

They were on the road, going up to Jerusalem, and Jesus was walking on ahead of them . . .

Jesus walked on ahead, leading the way up the hill to Jerusalem, and ultimately to Calvary. But after firmly fixing this image of Jesus leading the way, the writer shifts his focus to those following along behind, the disciples and the rest of the throng. We who follow Him as elders in shepherding the local church would be wise to take notice. Mark continues:

> . . . and they were amazed, and those who followed were fearful. And again He took the twelve aside and began to tell them what was going to happen to Him.

Leaders: amazed and afraid

For those of us who wish to lead by following Christ, we can expect two things: often we will be amazed; at times we will be afraid. We will be amazed because He *will* lead if we let Him—and His leadership will be far richer and more profound than our own. We will be amazed as we watch Him build a house that none could envision, because He does beyond what we ask or think. We will be amazed to see how well He leads the church that bears His name when we trust in His leadership and lordship, relinquishing our own fevered control.

But it is exactly this loss of control that will cause us to be afraid. When we lead by attempting to cling to control, we might ensure that nothing crazy begins to happen. We can refrain from making waves with the various power blocs in the church. We may shore up our own bases of power and perpetuate our tenure in office. We can minimize risk and keep the wildcards hidden deep within our stacked deck.

Leadership by our own control is not life-giving, but it is understandable. It is, to our human way of thinking, security.

The fear that makes us want to seize control is normal. The weight of the responsibility that leadership brings can easily bury us. We have two choices in handling that fear: give in to it, either by seizing control ourselves or allowing another to seize control; or walk through it, fixing our mind on Christ and His sovereign leadership.

If we choose the latter, we learn that fear is part of the package of eldership—a companion along the journey. But we cannot let fear replace Christ as our leader along the path.

Even those who followed Jesus while He dwelt with them found themselves being fearful, precisely because they were not in control—*He* was. Furthermore, He made it clear that the trip to Jerusalem would not be a joyful one. While in Galilee, just a few days prior to the uphill journey, Jesus had warned the disciples:

> **The Son of Man is to be delivered into the hands of men, and they will kill Him; and when He has been killed, He will rise three days later.**
>
> *Mark 9:31*

From a human perspective, the entire trip was a death march. The disciples fought hard against the idea that God's plan would take their leader to His death. "Not so, Lord," said Peter (Matthew 16:22). They, as we do, tried to control their lives to avoid the fear of death—the ultimate loss of control.

But Jesus' leadership showed no fear of death. He saw the end of the journey beyond the tomb at the right hand of the Father. As He yielded to His Father's will, He readily embraced a total loss of personal control.

No wonder the disciples were fearful as they followed Him! Had we been there, we would have been afraid too. True followers of Jesus Christ will occasionally walk in fear. If we do not, then we have not really given Him complete control but are leading in our own strength.

Thus, Mark gives us two measurements of authentic biblical eldership: *amazement* and *fear*. Amazement at the leading of Christ through the Spirit indwelling and empowering each elder. And fear because no man is visibly in control. There is no king, but there is *the* King. There is no organizational chart, but there is *His* organization. It is unlike anything found in any leadership handbook or business school. This is what makes biblical eldership exciting—and exasperating.

When we neglect to give control to Jesus, we lose more than our sense of amazement and fear. By succumbing to the temptation to jockey for position and power, we fail to see the eternal big picture. Mark provides us with an excellent example. Jesus, seeking to prevent the disciples from lapsing into the cadence of business as usual, reminds the disciples that this walk will end in suffering. But it will be translated into glory three days later.

> **And again He took the twelve aside and began to tell them what was going to happen to Him, saying, "Behold, we are going up to Jerusalem, and the Son of Man will be delivered to the chief priests and the scribes; and they will condemn Him to death, and will deliver Him to the Gentiles. And they will mock Him and spit upon Him, and scourge Him, and kill Him, and three days later He will rise again."**
>
> *Mark 10:32–34*

The disciples seemed to hear nothing of this dire warning! The text does not say, "Then the disciples were filled with foreboding," nor does it say, "Then the disciples began questioning Him concerning these things." No. Instead, the scene abruptly changes to focus on two disciples planning their political future (v. 35).

How often do we as elders fail to listen to Christ, and revert instead to our political planning to get ahead?

As Jesus walked on ahead, leading the way, James and John planned their next step independent from Him. Matthew, Mark, and Luke, the three synoptic writers, offer different perspectives in the telling of this story. In Matthew 20:17–22, the mother of

James and John led them to Jesus to request the best seats for her sons in Jesus' kingdom.

In Luke 18:34, we see that the whole group misunderstood the talk of crucifixion.

Mark reveals how James and John pulled away from the others to plan their future together. Perhaps they thought Jesus' kingdom would be inaugurated after a firestorm of judgment. They wrongly focused on their own position in His glorious kingdom. Where would they sit? What would their legacy be? How could they exercise the influence that was their due as two of the top three aides-de-camp? To allay their fears about their future position and power, they selfishly reached for the lever of control.

Who has not seen an elder respond this way? Our work and our achievement—our legacy—is on our minds. We want to make a mark, have great influence, and be seen as authoritative.

James and John fell into this classic pitfall—they quit listening to Christ and following His leadership and focused on their own power, position, and legacy. Worse yet, they tried to manipulate Jesus Christ, treating him with the same hocus-pocus that idol worshipers had been trying for centuries. If they got to Him first, maybe they could manage the outcome and control their legacy. But they had to move quickly—always a sign of the flesh, not of the Spirit.

Mark understates their self-elevating move in verse 35:

> **And James and John, the two sons of Zebedee, *came up to Him,* saying to Him, "Teacher, we want You to do for us whatever we ask of You."** (emphasis added)

Jesus is walking on ahead, leading the way, as James and John huddle together and whisper a plan for their own benefit. Then they gather up their robes and run ahead of their brothers to ask Jesus to elevate them above all the others. They hoped to come up to His level and be more mightily used by Him than anyone else, thus securing their share of the glory along the way.

What is striking about their power play is its total lack of subtlety. In plain view of the others, they ran ahead to walk with the Lead Man. When they got there, they blurted out a statement that would make any leader pause—a demand for "carte blanche." Furthermore, they tried to manipulate Him, using a formal title that denied their intimate friendship of three years. They approached Him as if they were beggars in the street, instead of beloved friends. They were working Him: "Teacher, we want You to do for us whatever we ask of You."

What a misstep! Their request defines elder leadership by the flesh, as opposed to leadership by Christ through the Spirit.

Leadership by the flesh has two mantras: "we want" (a coalition) or "I want" (one person pushing his agenda). James and John were rushing up ahead, trying to get the best of their brothers, taking control of an otherwise scary situation, and it was all based on the fleshly principle of "we want." Oh, how that conversation might have been different had they begun by asking what their Lord, their true leader, wanted! Leadership by the Spirit asks only one question: "Lord, what do *You* want?"

But in spite of their flesh on parade, Jesus answers them with characteristic patience, saying simply, "What do you want Me to do for you?"

This is God's patented method of dealing with human flesh. From the beginning in the Garden, when God asked Adam, "Where are you?" to the day when God asked Cain, "Where is Abel your brother?" to that lonely mountain where God asked Elijah, "What are you doing here, Elijah?" our God loves to ask the gentle but searching question. As James and John were trying to work the system, Jesus gently asked the searching question that could have revealed their selfish plot had they listened to it.

Second only to the folly of "we want" is the mistake of "we are able." "We want" is the motive of the flesh; "we are able" is the subtle pride of the flesh. Mark reveals this in verses 37–39:

And they said to Him, "Grant that we may sit in Your glory, one on Your right, and one on Your left." But Jesus said to them, "You do not know what you are asking for. Are you able to drink the cup that I drink, or to be baptized with the baptism with which I am baptized?" And they said to Him, "We are able."

Here Jesus simultaneously reveals both their ignorance and one of the chief principles of biblical eldership. He reveals their ignorance by plainly telling them, "You do not know what you are asking for." Jesus was the only true leader, and His path was leading toward the cross. That is the path for all who will lead by following Him—to the cross, and beyond the tomb. The way leads to Golgotha, not to glory—at least not in the short run.

James and John wanted the ecstasy without the agony. They wanted to share in His glory without having to share in His suffering. But in Jesus' mind the two are inextricably linked. By isolating the glory and craving it, they revealed their ignorance of this fact: the leadership that follows Christ follows Him right to the cross, then beyond to the resurrection and the glory.

Envisioning their future glory opened the door to their pride. Despite Jesus' clear rebuke, they tuned Him out and said, "We are able." Small wonder that only a few days later Jesus taught them about the vine and the branches in the upper room. Christ destroyed the myth of "we are able" with this simple truth:

I am the vine, you are the branches; he who abides in Me, and I in him, he bears much fruit; for apart from Me you can do nothing.

John 15:5

In Mark, Jesus doesn't even acknowledge the subtle pride of "we are able." He simply tells them what lies ahead on their road—namely death.

And Jesus said to them, "The cup that I drink you shall drink; and you shall be baptized with the baptism with which I am baptized . . ."

Mark 10:39

Then He burst their balloon:

. . . "but to sit on My right or on My left, this is not Mine to give; but it is for those for whom it has been prepared."

Mark 10:40

All that planning for nothing! The only immediate result of their plan was to incite jealousy and indignation in their brothers:

And hearing this, the ten began to feel indignant with James and John.

Mark 10:41

How true this is! Coalitions built on the shaky pillars of "we want" and "we are able" produce conflict. Sibling rivalry fractures the brotherhood.

Peter was likely the angriest, being the only member of the inner circle of three to be left out of the scheme. James and John were trying to erect a pyramid with themselves as close to the top as possible. And their brothers in lesser positions on the organizational chart were not happy.

What a mess along the road to Jerusalem! And how this kind of mess has permeated the church. Church politics, power plays, informal and even institutional hierarchies, and the never-ending jockeying for glory and position is pervasive in the church. This is why Jesus stopped in His tracks, called the men to Himself, and revealed to them the principle of leadership within His kingdom:

And calling them to Himself, Jesus said to them, "You know that those who are recognized as rulers of the Gentiles lord it over them; and their great men exercise authority over them. But it is not so among you, but whoever wishes to become great among you shall be your servant; and whoever wishes to be first among you shall be slave of all. For even the Son of Man did not come to be served, but to serve, and to give His life a ransom for many."

Mark 10:42–45

Here Jesus compares and defines worldly leadership methods with those of His Kingdom. He begins with the words, "You know . . . ." He starts from the familiar—something they know. Jesus may have been referring to the line-authority inherent in every hierarchical system of organization, such as a fishing business. But He also may have been referring to something the disciples were more painfully aware of—the iron hierarchy of the Roman political and military system.

The "great men," the strong men, the power players among the Gentiles led others by "lording it over them." They pulled rank, they employed strong-arm tactics, they intimidated, and, on the basis of the power vested in them by their office, by their riches, or by their military might, they commanded. The chattel beneath them had better obey, or else.

There was not a man among all the disciples who did not know this form of leadership, and who did not despise it. The very fact that they followed Jesus demonstrated how much they hated the status quo under Rome and Herod. Jesus gave the disciples both a warning and a new vision.

The warning was this: beware of becoming like the power-mongers whose abuse of power you have grown to hate. The power play of James and John was no different than the political intrigue swirling around Herod's palace. Fighting for position, manipulating others, and being jealous of those who were smarter or quicker was well known in the Roman legions. Yet the disciples were playing the same games, even though they were men who despised the domineering fist of Roman rule in Palestine.

There is a deep truth here for all elders. Most of us became devoted to eldership as a form of church leadership by painfully observing other forms of church government—such as the senior pastor model, congregational rule by majority vote, rigid denominational hierarchies, bishops in charge of geographic regions. Those forms of leadership are often rife with politics, because they are similar to worldly forms of organizational design.

Indeed, even though eldership is a flat organizational structure of brothers, with no dominant individual, there is always the danger of lapsing into the political power play, even with those who are ostensibly following Jesus' lead. One of the great ironies of leadership by the flesh is that it usually ends up resembling the form of leadership it rebelled against initially.

Anatomy of a church split

We have all seen how easily politics can split a church and then make the splinter-church as unhealthy as the original version. We know of one church formed after an ugly split with a political senior pastor of one of the largest churches in town. This new group adopted an elder form of church government to ensure no one individual ran the show.

Yet within six years, one man on the elder board was dictating the board's every move. By manipulating the flow of information, and by his absolute confidence that he was always right, he had muscled his way to a dominant position, much as Diotrophes had done in the cultural setting of 3 John.

Within six years, because these elders had not successfully reviewed one another and held this man in check, these dear men who had rebelled against the rigid control of one lone man were now being controlled by another lone man. The warning to us is clear. If we hate how powerful political leaders wield their unhealthy domination, we can't play power politics ourselves, nor can we stand idly by while others try to dominate.

Thankfully all of us have also seen godly men humbly serving despite the politics swirling around them, despite the gossip and backbiting—dear men who have our deepest respect as unsung heroes.

But more important than this warning in Mark 10 is Jesus' revolutionary new vision. He begins with, "But it is not so among you . . . ." Jesus did not say, "But it should not be so among you . . ." nor did He say, "Take all precaution to guard against this, lest it be so among you . . ." Rather, He said, "It is not so among you." Why is this?

It is because we already have our lead man—Jesus Christ! He is in charge, even when we do everything we can to overlook this fact. With Christ in charge, the whole issue of power and position is forever settled. He holds all power and authority over all things on earth and in heaven. All authority belongs to Him. We are simply called upon to serve Him and do what He desires.

Any attempt to grab power on our part is usurpation. It is stealing from Jesus Christ. We are never to attempt to secure power in any way. Jesus Christ has all power. Jesus Christ is the only one with whom absolute power does not corrupt absolutely. All power and authority rests with Him in all righteousness. This is not due to any power play but because of the simple truth that "Even the Son of Man did not come to be served, but to serve, and to give His life a ransom for many" (Matthew 20:28).

The power and authority of Jesus Christ emanated not only from His resurrection but also from the servanthood that preceded it on the cross. The most powerful thing Jesus ever did was to lay down His will in Gethsemane and allow Himself to be crucified. In that apparent powerlessness was the power of crucifixion love, the most potent force in the universe. In that act of seeming powerlessness, Jesus defeated death and crushed Satan's head. From that act of perfect loving sacrifice comes His authority to be called our Lord and Master.

Real power rests in Christ's self-sacrificial act of servanthood on the cross. Only when Christ lives within us and through us can we serve sacrificially and potently as elders in the church.

Our journey of following Christ as elders means allowing Him to serve and lead through us. We can permit no thoughts about politics, power, personal advancement, glory, or legacy. It must be all about Him and what He wants. He must be enough for us, and His desires must be ours.

As soon as we entertain the "we want" or "we are able" mantras, we have taken our eyes off our Lead Man. Our leadership is leadership on its knees—kneeling in prayer, humbly submitting to His will, kneeling to wash the feet of His sheep in our local church.

This is a much better image of biblical leadership. It is one of leadership on its knees. It was just such a leader that a Quaker farmer stumbled upon at Valley Forge during the Revolutionary War. Consider the following story:

> *During the Revolutionary War, when Americans were fighting for their freedom, the British Army captured Philadelphia. . . . The fall of Philadelphia was a great blow to the Americans, for in those days it was the capital of the new nation. But George Washington's army was not strong enough to stop the British forces. Once the King's men were inside the city, the only thing the American general could do was see that they did not get into the countryside to do any mischief. So Washington led his men to Valley Forge, a place just a few miles from Philadelphia. There the American army could spend the winter. It could defend itself if attacked, and it could keep close watch on the British.*

It would have been easier to fight many battles than to spend that winter in Valley Forge. It was December, and there was no shelter of any kind. The soldiers bravely set to work, building huts for themselves. They made them out of whatever they could find: logs, or fence rails, or just mud and straw. The snow drifted in at the windows, for they had no glass. The cold rain dripped through the roofs, the wind howled through every crack. There were few blankets, and many men slept shivering on the hard ground. Sometimes they sat up all night, crowding around the fires to keep from freezing. Their clothing was worse than their shelter. The whole army was in rags. Many of the men had no shirts. Even more were without shoes. Wherever they walked, the snow was marked with their blood. Some cut strips from their precious blankets, and wound them about their feet to protect them from the freezing ground. Food was scanty. Sometimes for several days, the soldiers went without meat. Sometimes they went even without bread. Around the camp, the groans of men who were sick and starving filled the air. Every evening when the sun sank, the officers wondered if the army could hold together one more day.

One cold day, a Quaker farmer was walking along a creek at Valley Forge, when he heard the murmur of a solemn voice. Creeping in its direction, he discovered a horse tied to a tree, but no rider. The farmer stole nearer, following the sound of the voice. Through a thicket, he saw a lone man, on his knees in the snow. It was General Washington. His cheeks were wet with tears as he prayed to the Almighty for help and guidance. The farmer quietly slipped away.

When he reached home, he said to his wife, "Hannah, my dear, all is well. The Americans will win their independence. George Washington will succeed."

"What makes thee think so, Isaac?" she asked.

"I have heard him pray, Hannah, out in the woods today," he said. "If there is anyone on this earth the Lord will listen to, it is this brave man. He will listen, Hannah, rest assured. He will."

The farmer was right. When at last the harsh winter melted away, and a soft green crept over the hillsides, George Washington's army still lived. Against all odds, it had outlasted the cruel Valley Forge snows. With new hope, the patriots marched away behind their brave commander, to fight the British and win their freedom. ("Prayer at Valley Forge," The Children's Book of Heroes, *edited by William Bennett.)*

Here was a godly leader who was literally in the trenches—a man of tears, kneeling in the snow to pray for those in his charge, looking to Christ and not himself.

Jesus was doing something entirely different than what the disciples thought along that journey upward to Jerusalem. He was on track to die and, by dying, to save the world. The disciples were failing to listen to Him, making political plans, and growing jealous and competitive. They were missing every point.

Yet our Lord of grace is so great that He even used their bumbling to His glory—He used their folly as an occasion for delivering His greatest word on leadership.

What a curious statement on God's creative grace. He drew His greatest portrait of eldership against the backdrop of a group of bumblers—men just like us.

He still walks on ahead—leading the way. The fact that He leads has not changed. Our job is to follow, eyes fixed on our Lead Man, leading on our knees, looking for opportunities to serve.

Chapter Two

Calling, Selection & Qualifications of Elders

After twenty years in the Bay area, I thought I would remain there ministering to a growing group of friends and a familiar congregation until the Rapture. However, the Lord arranged to move my wife and me from the San Francisco peninsula to the Northwest, specifically, Spokane in eastern Washington. What a surprise to leave a well-established church and longtime friends to arrive in a significantly different culture with a small church that had been created from a merger of two even smaller churches!

Our new church was governed by a group of eighteen men and women who sincerely wanted the Lord to build His church but were unsure about how this should be done. Several had been eld-ers in other churches, and through their influence a shift toward an elder form of government was underway. However, there were some in the church who questioned whether spiritual elders "knew enough" and had "enough experience" to be the sole governing board of a modern church. Points were raised like:

- How will the women's point of view be represented? (The rumor was circulating that there would be no women elders.)

- What about financial oversight? Surely we need experienced and objective business people to be sure pastors and elders don't do foolish things with the church's money.

- We ought to separate the spiritual oversight of the church from the business oversight. That is, it's all right for elders to take care of the spiritual side but we need professionals on the business side. This point was often mentioned when talk of building a church facility was discussed. At that time, the congregation met in a rented Seventh Day Adventist church. However, the church did own ten acres of well-located land.

But the question I had was: "How was the Lord going to sort all this out and what did He want me to do?" As I attended my first leadership meetings, I had the strong conviction that the Lord wanted me to keep quiet. It wasn't long before I observed that almost everyone was in agreement that the church should have a board of elders, plus a temporary leadership group to help get things started in a biblical manner. At that point I was asked to be an elder. To everyone's surprise I said no.

"Why not?" they asked. "After all, you were an elder at an other church for eighteen years."

"Because I don't qualify," I replied.

"Why? Is there some dark secret we don't know about?"

"No," I said, "it's because I don't meet, at this moment, one of the requirements from 1 Timothy 3:1–7."

So we began studying the qualifications as presented in the following passages of Scripture.

It is a trustworthy statement; if any man aspires to the office of overseer, it is a fine work he desires to do. An overseer, then, must be above reproach, the husband of one wife, temperate, prudent, respectable, hospitable, able to teach, not addicted to wine or pugnacious, but gentle, uncontentious, free from the love of money. He must be one who manages his own household well, keeping his children under control with all dignity (but if a man does not know how to manage his own household, how will he take care of the church of God?); and not a new convert, lest he become conceited and fall into the condemnation incurred by the devil. And he must have a good reputation with those outside the church, so that he may not fall into reproach and the snare of the devil.

1 Timothy 3:1–7

For this reason I left you in Crete, that you might set in order what remains, and appoint elders in every city as I directed you, namely, if any man be above reproach, the husband of one wife, having children who believe, not accused of dissipation or rebellion. For the overseer must be above reproach as God's steward, not self-willed, not quick-tempered, not addicted to wine, not pugnacious, not fond of sordid gain, but hospitable, loving what is good, sensible, just, devout, self-controlled, holding fast the faithful word which is in accordance with the teaching, that he may be able both to exhort in sound doctrine and to refute those who contradict.

Titus 1:5–9

Be on guard for yourselves and for all the flock, among which the Holy Spirit has made you overseers, to shepherd the church of God which He purchased with His own blood.

Acts 20:28

Therefore, I exhort the elders among you, as your fellow-elder and witness of the sufferings of Christ, and a partaker also of the glory that is to be revealed, shepherd the flock of God among you, not under compulsion, but voluntarily, according to the will of God; and not for sordid gain, but with eagerness; nor yet as lording it over those allotted to your charge, but proving to be examples of the flock.

1 Peter 5:1–3

From these passages we sorted out the following qualifications in terms of attributes, attitudes, and activities.

Attributes:

- above reproach, blameless—not open to censure, irreproachable, no charge can be brought against him that will stick

- one-wife man—physically and mentally faithful to one woman

- temperate, not a drunkard— never out of control, not addicted to wine

- sensible, self-controlled—displays common sense in personal actions, controls his passions, balanced, discreet, reasonable

- not a novice, not a recent convert—maturing in doctrine and experience, not a brand new Christian

- well thought of by outsiders, good reputation with outsiders—pays bills promptly, gets along with neighbors, demonstrates wisdom in his relationship with nonbelievers, bears a good, consistent testimony before the world

- examples to the flock—displays godliness in his actions, is transparent about God's work in his life

Attitudes:

- dignified, respectable—maintains well-arranged life, orderly, decorous, disciplined, honorable

- hospitable, lover of strangers—opens home for hospitality, reaches out to strangers

- not arrogant, not violent—not contentious, doesn't have a chip on his shoulder, a peaceable man

- not quarrelsome—never in your face, willing to yield in arguments, doesn't demand his rights, not a fighter

- not a lover of money or eager for gain—not a wheeler-dealer or a manipulator, content with God's provision

- willing to serve, eager for service—volunteers with his whole heart, willing to do the unnoticed service

- not lording it over others, not domineering—not bossy, demanding, overbearing, or claiming authority over others

- must render an account—responsible to the Lord as his boss in everything, demonstrates a spirit of submissiveness

Activities:

- apt to teach and feed the flock, hold firm the sure Word, give instruction, able to refute opposers—has the spiritual gift of teaching and uses it, the Word is a cornerstone of his life

- overseer, shepherds the flock, guards the flock—evaluates spiritual needs, helps people discover spiritual gifts, warns against spiritual perils, counsels, guides, protects the flock from spiritual dangers

- manages home well, keeps children under control, respectable—employs wise home management, spiritual leader of his home, displays godly characteristics to family

As we went through the attributes, I pointed out that I didn't meet the sixth and seventh of these since I had just arrived in town. Time was needed to develop a local reputation with outsiders and to provide an example to the flock. The elders agreed. I wasn't considered for eldership until after my first year had passed.

Remember that part about me keeping quiet? Well, the Lord used His Word (as we all were examining it each week) to convince individual members of the leadership group that they shouldn't be governing the church. No one was pushed. These good people gradually became comfortable with the idea of appointing biblically qualified elders to govern this specific church. The women also decided this was a good thing. Now the Lord did move several families out of our fellowship, but without pressure and for different reasons. Fascinating! Finally we reached a point where the key question was asked: "Who specifically has the Holy Spirit already made overseers of the flock of this church?"

Someone suggested putting all potentially qualified persons before the congregation for a vote. The only problem was that it had taken us more than six months of study to understand the basic qualifications for eldership. How could we get the whole congregation up to speed so that they could vote intelligently?

In addition, our congregation had a significant percentage of "baby" Christians, about a third, who were just getting started in the faith. Another 40 percent were "young" Christians, growing in the faith. Then perhaps there were 20 percent who were "mature" Christians. Finally, we had a percentage whom we believed weren't Christians at all. It would take a miracle for the Holy Spirit to get this congregation to vote for biblically qualified elders only, since so few were mature believers and able to discern between spiritual qualifications and a popularity contest. In the end, the whole leadership group agreed unanimously to examine each member in light of what we had learned.

Immediately one woman said, "I don't qualify, because the text says an elder must be husband of one wife." After considerable discussion, we decided that was indeed the biblical norm.

One by one, everyone was examined. Most took themselves out of the picture because they recognized they did not meet one or more of the criteria. All were certain that none of us meet the qualifications in an absolute sense. We all are on the way to *becoming*. Therefore, we needed one more identifier to help us. In Acts 20:28 the apostle Paul tells the elders at Ephesus that the "Holy Spirit made you overseers." We drew from that statement the concept that there should be evidence of the Holy Spirit's work. So we asked:

"Are people in the congregation already being shepherded by this man?"

"Are people following this man's leadership?"

"Are people being fed spiritually by this man's teaching?"

These questions were very helpful, and we finished the process with everyone agreeing on four men. These four were then presented to the congregation with a statement that said:

"We, the about-to-be-dissolved leadership group, believe these four men are elders that the Lord has appointed for this church. If anyone has definable cause to question this belief, please let us know immediately."

Thus, God graciously used us to establish an elder-led church. Almost immediately the elders decided four things:

- Elders, together with the pastoral staff, should study God's Word on a regular basis. Every other week should be a meeting for study. We embarked on a comprehensive study on "What elders need to know." (See Appendix II, p. 197).

- Every study meeting would have a prayer time set aside for the specific concerns and needs of individuals in the Body.

- Every elder would be evaluated once every eighteen months by all the other elders and pastoral staff. (See chapter 11, p. 161).

- The basic responsibility for each elder is to ascertain the mind of the Lord for this church and make all decisions unanimously with the other elders. (See chapter 8, p. 127.)

Looking back over the last ten years, it's fair to ask how things have worked out. The following impressed me most in regard to our new elder-led church.

Within months one of the teaching pastors resigned from both his position as co-preaching pastor and elder because of family issues. Suddenly we had major problems to deal with. It seemed like the elders were in the middle of a raging river, swimming for dear life. Why didn't the Lord just give them some simple problems to start with?

The Lord knew exactly what He was doing, because no amount of human wisdom could have been adequate for the leadership task they faced. As I watched these men wrestle with the issues week after week, I saw them become absolutely certain that Jesus was the only one who was in charge. He alone was capable of leading them to the end result that He wanted. Many times the moderator would say, "Fellows, we don't have unanimity on this issue. Go home and pray that God will give us a solution." One week later, they would find themselves in agreement because the Holy Spirit had worked in each one's heart and mind, independent of any other elder.

The second thing I observed was that God was in the business of maturing individual elders. The men displayed a hunger to know God. They developed a strong desire to understand how God works in human affairs. There was a seriousness about studying the Word. All these things became increasingly evident as these dear men struggled through the tough issues. A year went by and I joined them officially as an elder and learned and grew as they did.

Soon another tough issue presented itself to the elders—the building. Building your own house can put a real strain on a marriage. Building a new church facility has similar effects for elders.

We started with the financial side. What had the Lord given us already?

- We owned ten acres (paid for);
- We had a building fund of about $300,000;
- We were paying $1500 rent per month for facilities.

Our first concern was to avoid true debt. We defined this to be "having a large mortgage on the facilities which could not be easily covered by a sale of the property." We also took note of James 4:13–16 where God warns about predicting the future in financial matters. After time spent asking the Lord for wisdom together and individually, we reached unanimity on the following parameters:

- any mortgage obligation could not exceed 33 percent of the fair market value of the project;

- the monthly obligation should be close to the current average monthly giving for the building fund plus the rent.

Our next task was to get an idea of what size facility would fit us and at what cost. We were consistently filling the current building to capacity. After consultation with several church architects, we learned that a modest church building, slightly larger than the one we were currently using, would cost more than a million dollars. This was clearly outside our second parameter.

Now what?

As we sought the mind of the Lord we decided to move on two fronts.

First, we would tell the whole story to the congregation and ask them to talk to the Lord about the building and their giving for it.

Second, we would invite eight ministry teams to design a multipurpose structure that would serve as a tool for their ministries.

It seemed clear that the Lord was working, because more than $100,000 came in during the next year and the ministry teams developed a serviceable floor plan. There was an attitude of cooperation in the process. It was an exciting meshing of needs and space availability. The conviction began to grow: maybe God was going to work this out after all!

The design was a challenge. No one wanted a "light industrial" look, and yet we knew that an expensive traditional church building wasn't going to be feasible. Eventually, the Lord led us to a commercial builder who had a reputation for integrity and innovation. Their architect was easy to work with. After many hours of interaction we had a plan for a multipurpose facility that was attractive, met our ministry needs, was reasonably acceptable to the county, and was close to our financial parameter.

One thing which made this workable was the decision to do some of the work ourselves and act as our own general contractor. There were concerns, of course: Could we really do this without creating a mess? Would the people work hard at hanging drywall, putting up trim, installing finished plumbing? But the Lord kept bringing us to unanimous decisions, though there were times I was certain that we would never come to a decision at all.

I am convinced that the Lord was building people through this whole process. Men got to know other men by working side by side, high up on extension platforms, hanging drywall. Women helped each other staining doors, painting rooms, cleaning windows. It seemed everyone had a hand in the creation of the building. In the end it was finished to God's glory with a majority of the congregation participating.

Here is a summary of the decisions we believe the Lord led us to make:

- Set a sound financial parameter.
- Have ministry teams design the building layout.
- Communicate with the congregation throughout the process.
- Involve as many as possible in the actual construction work.
- Trust Him to get us through problems as they showed up.

The final results were as follows:

- An attractive 16,000 square-foot multipurpose facility
- A $54/sq.ft. total occupancy cost (including landscaping and parking lot)
- A mortgage at 28 percent of the project's fair market value.
- A monthly payment in line with our previous experience.

In addition, the whole congregation was amazed at what God had done. The executives from the construction company were unusually pleased with this project, and many people from the community expressed approval.

Of course, the greatest result was that God was honored and glorified. We believe that this happened because we as a local Body of believers were willing to take God at His Word and do His work His way. That is, by the grace of God we studied His Word and sought to know and practice His principles and standards for godly leaders. To the degree that we obeyed those principles and standards, to that same degree God blessed our church family. And when we did not obey, we did not enjoy His blessing.

Blessing, success, growth, the maturing of God's people, and most importantly, God's Name is honored and glorified. All can occur when we are willing to follow His instructions. This vital truth will become evident in our next chapter.

CHAPTER THREE

Elders In Balance: Hard Minds, Soft Hearts

As a college student, I became fascinated by eldership when I had the opportunity to watch a godly group of elders in action. I was the greenest of greenhorns, attending Stanford University, and full of zeal for Jesus Christ to whom I had committed my life only one year earlier. I had become the college pastor's right-hand man, and he had invited me to attend an elder meeting with him—a smart discipleship choice on his part.

I came into the room and was met by the men. They were cracking jokes and chuckling together. Most were gray-hairs, but a few were in their thirties and forties. Here were the men I observed: Bob, one of the five founding elders of the church and a magnificent man in his thirty-sixth year of service; Ray, the founding pastor and world-renowned expositor in his thirty-fourth year of service; Bob, an elder with strong teaching gifts; Paul, whose leadership and wisdom gifts were legendary; Barney, an executive from the airline industry whose hands-on shepherding as an elder was a model of servant leadership; Craig, a financial wizard who served as treasurer and whose integrity was impeccable; Bruce, a businessman whose home was almost the second campus of the church; Eff, an investment banker with outstanding gifts of leadership; Steve, a faithful pastor with a strong teaching gift; Don, a quiet but godly shepherd with the gift of mercy; Bill, a company president with a passion for elder leadership and outstanding leadership gifts; and Don, a younger elder with solid gifts of teaching and leadership. Twelve men in all—not a bad number. The room also included several visitors, including the college pastor and me, since the meetings were always open unless a sensitive issue was under discussion.

I watched the moderator set the meeting in motion. Surprisingly, he was one of the youngest men on the elder team. He began with a Bible study, because he said it was crucial to start by sitting under the authority of the Word of God. The study was followed by a time when the elders prayed for different members of the Body and the issues on the agenda.

Most compelling for me was to watch the older men treat the younger ones with respect and honor. This deference was immediately returned by the younger elders.

As the meeting progressed, discussion was lively. Things occasionally ground to a halt after a bold, passionate statement by one of the men. The more forceful personalities spoke often, but the quieter ones were asked to share what the Spirit was putting on their heart regarding the issue at hand. The men were discussing the Sunday evening Body Life service, whether or not it should be continued. At one point, they asked my opinion as a college student. When I shared my opinion, they listened and nodded. My word had weight. There was a sense of equality and a total absence of political jockeying that made this meeting utterly unique in my experience. The men were not concerned about themselves or their own pet programs—they came together on a quest. Their quest was to know and understand the mind of Christ on each issue. A nobler quest cannot be found.

The Body Life discussion was tabled that night. Each man was charged to pray about it and ask the Lord if the season for that service was over for now. Then, other items were addressed.

Again, the discussion was lively, and each man was asked to share how God was leading him on the subject. Then a vote was taken. There was a godly solemnity to the process. Voting was not done by acclamation, or as a passing concession to Robert's Rules of Order. The secretary polled each man by name, and each elder stated what the Lord had put on his heart. It was clear that each had wrestled with God and reached an individual decision. Each man acted according to the power of his convictions. As the vote proceeded, the amazing unanimity of the mind of Christ gradually appeared. I remember a sense of awe coming over me. God had visibly moved within these men. The decision of twelve men spoke with one voice. It was a unanimous decision that revealed the mind of Christ.

I left that meeting with a sense of having been on holy ground. I had never been treated with greater respect and courtesy. I had sensed their rest in Christ. I had heard their jokes and good-humored jibes at one another. I had heard them burst into hearty laughter. I had watched them start by studying the Scriptures and praying. I had seen each man have an independent voice before God, without coercion, both in the discussion and in that roll call vote. And when their unanimity was reached, a sense of confidence in their leadership filled my heart with excitement about the direction of the church. The Lord was in charge. He was actively leading His church. There was no other place on earth I wanted to be that night. I was hooked on eldership. Fifteen years later, and many good, bad, and ugly elder meetings since, I am still hooked.

Two overarching qualities defined those men: they were hard-minded and soft-hearted. With regard to issues and challenges, they were hard-minded. Each argument put forth had to be biblically sound, or one should get ready for some flak! But these men were remarkably soft-hearted—especially for being such strong leaders—when it came to individuals within the Body. It is exactly this balance of being hard-minded and soft-hearted in the Spirit that underlies the servant-leader elder.

A Matrix for Evaluating Elder Teams

For five years prior to becoming a pastor, I was a management consultant. Because of that, I often analyze issues by using two-by-two matrices. This can be a helpful tool in understanding the basic dynamics underlying more complex problems. Evaluating how an elder team is doing is very useful, but having a framework for evaluation is essential. Let's consider the following two-by-two matrix for evaluating elder teams:

	Hard-Minded	Soft-Minded
Soft-Hearted	BEST CASE	SOFT CASE
Hard-Hearted	HARD CASE	WORST CASE

Given this framework, elder teams can fall into four categories. The *best-case* scenario is the top left quadrant, where the elder team is primarily hard-minded and soft-hearted. The *hard-case* scenario is the bottom left quadrant, where the elder team is primarily hard-minded and hard-hearted. The *soft-case* scenario is the top right quadrant, where the elder team is primarily soft-minded and soft-hearted. And the *worst-case* scenario is the bottom right quadrant, where the elder team is primarily soft-minded and hard-hearted.

I have served with or observed elder teams from each of these four scenarios. On the following pages are profiles of the characteristics, strengths, and weaknesses of elder teams under each scenario. We will work our way up the scale, starting with the worst-case scenario and moving from there to the best-case.

Worst-case Scenario—Soft-Minded and Hard-Hearted

Characteristics: This elder team is usually characterized by faulty theology and hard-hearted dogmatism. These elders are often self-appointed, rather than men appointed by the Holy Spirit as were the Ephesian elders in Acts 20:28. They may have adopted elder-led church government as a reaction against an abusive, "one-man-show" senior pastor; thus, they may be anti-pastor but pro-elder.

This team will tend to "major on the minors," often creating a "unique" approach that may be subconsciously designed to make up for a lack of spiritual giftedness among key members of the team. For example, if one of the key men does not have a gift of preaching or teaching, he may lead the board to adopt a Sunday morning format that eliminates traditional preaching. The church might then opt for worship, sharing, and a five-minute sermonette at the end. The burden of the teaching might then be passed off to the Sunday school classes, which utilize a highly interactive approach geared to avoid traditional teaching. Such a tortured "vision," which starves the sheep by removing expository preaching from the Sunday morning menu, is actually driven by a lack of giftedness among the leaders. In this case, the elders are soft-minded about feeding the sheep regularly with God's Word.

Worse yet, there is usually a hard-hearted dogmatism that characterizes such a team. This team constantly emphasizes the "divine right" of elders—equating the elders' will with God's will. They frequently remind themselves that they are the only ones doing it right, and shake their heads at the way other people "do church." They rarely admit even the slightest error on their part, attacking anyone bold enough to call them to account. They are contentious, and lord it over the sheep. Fringe groups that eventually become cults are characterized by such soft-mindedness about Biblical truth and hard-heartedness about always being right.

Biblically speaking, they are men such as Ezekiel describes.

Son of man, prophesy against the shepherds of Israel. Prophesy and say to those shepherds, "Thus says the Lord GOD, 'Woe, shepherds of Israel who have been feeding themselves! Should not the shepherds feed the flock? You eat the fat and clothe yourselves with the wool, you slaughter the fat sheep without feeding the flock. Those who are sickly you have not strengthened, the diseased you have not healed, the broken you have not brought back, nor have you sought for the lost; but with force and with severity you have dominated them.'"

Ezekiel 34:2–4

Irenaeus also describes this type of eldership in *Against Heresies,* written between AD 182–188: "Those, however, who are believed to be presbyters [elders] by many, but serve their own lusts, and do not place the fear of God supreme in their hearts, but conduct themselves with contempt toward others, and are puffed up with the pride of holding the chief seat, and work evil deeds in secret, saying, 'No man sees us,' shall be convicted by the Word, who does not judge after outward appearance, nor looks upon the countenance, but the heart."

Even in the second century, the worst-case scenario existed!

Strengths: None.

Weaknesses: These men will be weak in theology, weak in gift-edness, insecure about their leadership, weak in grace, weak in admitting mistakes, weak in communication skills, weak in conflict-resolution skills, and generally unhappy. Since several, if not all, of the men are unqualified biblically, the elder review process will be weak, if it exists at all.

Unfortunately, wherever eldership gets a bad name, this can usually be traced back to worst-case scenario elder teams—soft-minded but hard-hearted. The abuses and oddities of such teams have convinced many that eldership cannot work. It can and does work, but not under this worst-case scenario. The faster we move on, the better!

Hard Case Scenario—Hard-Minded and Hard-Hearted

Characteristics: This elder team has a solid understanding of biblical theology, but is a primarily a team of administrators. They grasp the truth, but they apply it in a coldly efficient manner.

Elder teams like this will run the church as a business—by the numbers, by the book, and by the flesh. Their doctrinal statement is finely honed, with every nuance of biblical revelation neatly packaged. The office will be run like a well-oiled machine. Schedules will be strictly adhered to, and reviews of ministry successes will be evaluated by the numbers: growth at 7 percent annually, giving increased by 5 percent, and so forth. Woe to the pastor or ministry leader who doesn't post good numbers!

Unfortunately, this team and the church under their leadership are often cold and clinical. Token prayer is frequent, since leadership is all about marketing to the demographics and applying the right technique to the appropriate felt-need. Ministry programs abound, but ministries of real compassion, or ministries to those with messy problems like divorce or sexual addiction, are usually absent. Often there is an undercurrent of anger when things do not go as planned, and the dominant leadership style is passive-aggressive—the thin-lipped smile when things are going well, and the clenched jaw muscle when they are not. If one in the Body has a besetting sin and needs counsel, or if a child is beginning to rebel and his parents need a listening ear, this would be the next-to-last group of men one would call upon.

Biblically speaking, this elder team is probably most like the elders of the Sanhedrin in Jesus' day—guardians of the Torah who split every theological hair, but whose program in the Temple or whose expectations of what the Messiah will look like cannot be interrupted. They might pray like the Pharisee in Luke 18:11–12:

> **The Pharisee stood and was praying thus to himself, "God, I thank Thee that I am not like other people: swindlers, unjust, adulterers, or even like this tax-gatherer. I fast twice a week; I pay tithes of all that I get."**

In this prayer is a profound lack of compassion, and an emphasis on programs (fasting) and bondage to the numbers (the 10 percent tithe).

Strengths: This elder team's strengths lie in the areas of efficiency and running smooth operations. A church like this is rarely in serious financial trouble, and has a host of programs, because they manage according to those goals. A need to be in a controlled environment to feel safe might cause one to gravitate toward an elder team and church like this.

Weaknesses: The most glaring weakness will be revealed when mercy is needed, because compassion is virtually absent in this hard-case scenario. This elder team will rarely be approached by the weak or broken sheep, because the elders are rarely approachable. They have erected an immaculate ivory tower and are unwilling to roll up their sleeves and jump into the messy areas of ministry in the community. A person with a heart for the dimly burning wicks and bruised reeds, such as Jesus had, will not find a listening ear on this elder team. The hard case tends to break hearts: the hearts of the sheep and God's large heart as well.

Interestingly, there are not too many of these hard case elder-led churches around. The inefficiencies and slow timetables inherent in seeking and finding the mind of Christ prove too frustrating for administratively-oriented leaders. Thus these churches tend toward other types of church government.

Soft-case Scenario—Soft-Minded and Soft-Hearted

Characteristics: This elder team is the opposite of the hard case. The men here are gifted with gifts of mercy and serving, but are noticeably lacking in leadership or administrative skills. They haven't yet gotten around to writing a doctrinal statement, because they don't want to exclude anyone. Their accounting system will be messy at best, and financial reporting about hard numbers will be infrequent and unclear. The nursery program is in a shambles, because they don't want to draw up the hard-minded policies needed to ensure a safe and healthy environment for the little ones. They excel whenever someone in the Body has a sin problem to share, or needs compassion during a time of bereavement. They are often referred to as "good men, with good hearts," but many in the Body are continually frustrated by the obvious lack of leadership.

Furthermore, wolves who come begging money from the members of the Body, or who prey on some of the single women, are never confronted or asked to leave. In fact, citing the boundless compassion of Jesus, these elders will tend to focus their ministry on that wolf, hoping to bring him into the fold!

This elder team and the church led by them will be relaxed to the point of being rumpled, but they will be exceedingly warm and welcoming. Their heads will quickly nod with a knowing and compassionate glance when anyone begins to share their tale of personal woe. The emphasis in the church will be on coming to church to get healed, to find grace, and to soak up God's love. Often these elders will mask their laziness or inability to confront tough people or tough issues with a cloak of passive gentility. All manner of ugliness may be seething underneath the warm veneer of this church, because truth rarely gets spoken, and hidden sin finds fertile soil in which to grow.

Biblically speaking, these men may be exceedingly gracious but tolerate sin among the leadership as Eli did (1 Samuel 2:12–36). For years, Eli's sons slept with the women serving at the doorway of the tent of meeting, and they took the fat portions of the sacrifices for themselves. Eli didn't confront their sin and didn't speak the hard but necessary word.

In the end the Lord told Eli that he had honored his sons more than he had honored God. Eli was soft-minded when it came to responsibly following the details of the sacrifices and he was soft-hearted with his own sons. Eli honored his sons above the Lord. Elders in this soft case honor comfort above the Lord.

Strengths: This elder team is amazingly strong in supporting those with long-term illnesses, besetting sins, or abusive backgrounds. Their church may be a wonderful place to heal from past wounds, but it will not be a place to lay a solid foundation of truth upon which to grow for the future. If one has mercy or serving gifts, and is drawn to serve the hurting, one may well be drawn to this elder team and the church that reflects them.

Weaknesses: Before long, the chronic lack of leadership or good record-keeping will become evident, and many in the Body will be driven away by the rampant chaos. The easy-going approach to the church finances may leave the church vulnerable to financial trouble. Good folks with leadership gifts will find themselves quickly burning out, because they will be shouldering too much of the load themselves.

Elder-led churches with a reputation of being poorly led may have elders who are too soft-minded and soft-hearted to provide effective leadership. When leaders don't lead, sin and chaos are crouching behind every door.

Having looked at three cases which leave much to be desired, we will focus on the best-case scenario, since that is where we all want to be as elders.

Best-case Scenario—Hard-Minded and Soft-Hearted

Characteristics: This elder team can be characterized by one word: *balance.* It is comprised of men who have strong leadership and administrative gifts, as well as those with strong pastoring, serving, and mercy gifts. In the balance God achieves on this team, there is great wisdom—knowing how and when to make decisions, and knowing how and when to inform the Body of these decisions.

These men will be strong biblical leaders—strong in grace, strong in faith, and strong in the gentle meekness that serves others and treats everyone in the Body with equal value, just as Jesus did. In fact, this elder board is very much like Jesus Himself— holding the wise balance between vigorous, visionary leadership and gracious compassion.

The elder team I described from that first elder meeting at PBC is the best-case scenario I have ever seen. It was balanced in virtually every area—wise elders with over thirty years of service and vigorous younger elders in their early forties; strong leadership gifts combined with strong pastoring and mercy gifts; forceful "bottom liners" who had to restrain themselves from dominating the discussion and "quiet contemplators" who had to force themselves to speak up; successful businessmen and blue collar journeymen—in short, there was a wonderful overall balance of personalities and information-processing styles. When all these "opposites" came under the control of the Holy Spirit and a unanimous decision was revealed, the mind of Christ became evident in leading His church.

Biblically speaking, the most powerful illustration of this type of elder team at work is seen in Acts 15:1–29, at the famous Jerusalem Council. The debate rages, with impassioned input on both sides, until the Spirit gives James the word of wisdom. After James speaks, unanimity is reached when "it seemed good to the apostles and elders, with the whole church" to depart from the legalistic traditions of the Jews.

Strengths: When godly people allow the Holy Spirit to grace a church with a hard-minded, soft-hearted elder team, the fruit is boundless. The sheep will have great confidence in the leadership of Jesus Christ expressed through the eldership and there will be corresponding fruitfulness in the ministry. If there is strength in a multitude of counselors, there is even more strength in a multitude of strong elders united by the Spirit into a hard-minded but soft-hearted team.

Weaknesses: This type of team is hard to find in a local church, and it is difficult to maintain this level of excellence from one generation to the next. The Holy Spirit who makes elders has to perpetuate this best-case scenario, and He works in different ways in different generations.

But how does a group of elders strike the balance, being simultaneously hard-minded and soft-hearted? Rather than list some prescriptions, let me relate the following stories of elders who modeled hard-minded, soft-hearted behavior.

Adopting Missionaries

One church that impressed me took an innovative approach to missions. They "adopted missionaries," building a relational safety net around those who were part of the Body serving in a foreign field. For each missionary, a team was developed, which was headed by a pastor or elder who served as the key liaison, and included people within the Body who were committed to supporting the missionary in prayer and/or financially. This team was also committed to walking alongside the missionary by sending emails, letters, care packages, and information about the home church.

I was particularly impressed when one long-term missionary family serving in Asia went through a dark period of spiritual warfare and marital discord. The team surrounding them, headed up by an elder, immediately arranged for them to be flown back home, where they spent a number of months reunited with the Body that had adopted them. Several homes were made available to them so that they could live there as a family and heal, while the couple underwent some much-needed marital counseling.

That period in the family's life was not publicized; it was a time when the elders and the Body surrounded them with a quiet, serving love that allowed them to heal. After six months they returned to their foreign post.

The balance evident in this story is two-fold: the hard-mindedness recognizes that many traditional approaches to missions can leave missionaries high and dry during seasons of darkness, and it wisely sets up a support structure that admits the reality of those times and is quickly mobilized when the darkness comes. The soft-heartedness is manifold: the family was welcomed into their adoptive church family in short order, homes and funds were readily provided, counseling was supplied, children were befriended, and all of this happened with a bare minimum of damaging gossip. That was hard-minded but soft-hearted eldering.

Elders Praying for a Woman with Lung Cancer

Another moment that had a profound impact on me came on the night my wife and I took her mother to the elders for prayer and anointing with oil, according to James 5. About six months earlier God's loyal love led my mother-in-law to repentance, and she had accepted Christ. She now wanted to come to the elders as a new Christian in obedience to the Scriptures.

My mother-in-law had been coughing for over two years before she had been correctly diagnosed with cancer. Now she was undergoing chemotherapy. When we took her to the elders for prayer, she was wheeling along an oxygen tank to help her breathe. The elders loved our family, and knew the story about her recent conversion, so it was an emotional night for all of us.

Yet amid the tears, several of the men asked her some hard-minded questions. One man gently asked, "Do you have any unconfessed sin in your life?" It was a blunt question, one that could have been easily overlooked given the circumstances. Her reply was humble and contrite: "Not that I know of." She had been praying that God would help her see any sin that might contribute to her illness.

After the elders described to her the principles of James 5, they anointed her head with oil. Then there was a time of prayer, with the elders gathered around her and many laying hands on her. One of the elders, a rugged outdoorsman, got down on his knees in all humility to pray for her and to lean over and touch her shoulders. I will never forget those prayers; it was a touching and emotional moment.

Her cancer went into remission, and her oxygen tank was no longer necessary. But in the sovereignty of God, two months later a blood clot unrelated to her cancer lodged in her heart and she passed away. She was a woman who all her life had been treated poorly by men. But how the Lord blessed her that night through those elders! They treated her hard-mindedly as godly men, but soft-heartedly, according her a dignity and honor she had never received before. The power of hard-minded but soft-hearted eldering emanates from the manliest man of all, who similarly served the adulterous woman in John 8.

Evaluating a Fellow Elder

Perhaps the most essential time to be hard-minded but soft-hearted is at review time. Every elder and pastor ought to be rigorously evaluated every year or two. Reviews for the purpose of holding elders accountable are vital to the spiritual life of the Body. The elder is helped to see himself more clearly before the Lord, and the other men show that they love him enough to take on his evaluation.

One young church had recently added a new elder. He was a proven servant who for years had effectively spearheaded one of the mid-week children's programs at church. He was well-established in the community, and his wife and children loved the Lord. He was a beloved fixture at the church, primarily because of his selfless serving of the children. So, fitting all the character qualifications and with a track record of faithful servanthood, he was asked to be an elder.

But over the next two years, it became increasingly apparent that his spiritual gifts were service and helps, not necessarily the wisdom or leadership gifts required for an elder. Moreover, he was not apt to teach, having neither a great passion nor a great ability to teach the Scriptures. So, when it came time for him to undergo his review, the other men carefully prayed and did their homework, gathering feedback from the man himself, those on his ministry team, and others in the Body who knew him well. As the review process continued, a consensus started to emerge—he was gifted and qualified to serve as a deacon, but not as an elder.

This review was a proving ground for hard-minded but soft-hearted elders. All of them were in agreement about this man's giftedness and qualifications for ministering as a deacon.

Yet, there was risk involved in confronting him at the review. What if the man balked, or argued against the others? Since he was enormously popular among the Body, would there be a potential rift if he disagreed and built a coalition against the elders?

Casting these concerns aside, the elders hard-mindedly decided to tell him the truth, but to do so in a way that honored him and preserved his personal dignity. In a private meeting, one of the elders shared the unanimous conclusion of the other elders: that this man should be set free from the burden of shepherding the flock as an elder, and be committed to serving the Body as a deacon.

At first the elder was taken aback. This was not what he expected to hear. Undoubtedly he had to wrestle with his pride. But to his great credit, he yielded to the elders and graciously stepped off the elder team. Several years later, he told the elder who had approached him in private that they had been absolutely right, and that focusing on the deacon ministry God had given him had been the best decision he could have made. Because of a hard-minded but soft-hearted approach to the review process, this man was set free to serve God, making the best of all the gifts and abilities the Lord had given him. He served in the same capacity in the children's ministry for close to forty years.

A Defining Moment: Evaluating Spiritual Giftedness in Others

The proving ground of hard-minded but soft-hearted shepherding comes when elders are asked to evaluate the spiritual gifts of someone in the Body. While this may be fairly straightforward when the person in question is young, it is increasingly difficult if that person is a pastor under review. And it is most difficult for an elder who is serving outside his giftedness.

Elders must not ignore this issue. More than any other time in the life of the church, such moments call for honesty and gracious confrontation. The elders must hard-minded about this, but they must be wisely soft-hearted in communicating their assessments. This is especially true for the person who needs that feedback but has not asked for it.

In most churches, there is one key player ministering outside his area of giftedness. It may be an elder who left the business world to become a pastor but doesn't have the preaching or leadership gifts to justify his full-time ministry commitment. Or it may be an elder who should actually be serving as a deacon. It may be an elder who is gifted as an administrator but not as a shepherd, and whose lack of compassion for the sheep is painfully evident.

The hours of prayer, discussion, and soul-searching spent on the part of everyone in the church who senses that someone is out of place can't be counted. Usually, the elders have the problem diagnosed. Every elder knows that "so and so" is not gifted for what they are doing. But tackling the problem with the hard-minded truth about giftedness is one of the toughest tasks facing the elders. Often it is so tough that the subject is steadfastly avoided, like the proverbial emperor who has no clothes.

It is crucial for the elders to take up the mantle of hard-minded but soft-hearted leadership and to pray, gathering data methodically, and then privately but graciously confronting the brother or sister. This is love of the purest kind: speaking the truth in love, that all members of the Body may be built up (Ephesians 4:15–16).

The Litmus Test: Elders You Can Call On In the Day of Distress

The litmus test of elders who serve hard-mindedly but soft-heartedly is this: Do the sheep call them when they get into trouble?

Larry Crabb's astute observation in his book *The Silence of Adam* saddened me:

A young couple wrote me in desperation. "We've been married six years and it's just not working. Do you know a good Christian therapist in our area?" Why would this couple write to me, a trained, licensed, professional psychologist, rather than ask an elder in their church to meet with them? Were they drawn by my title? By my character? Why do most people with problems think immediately of getting "professional help"? Why don't they turn to wise Christian men and women? Most of us would no more consult an elder in our church for help with panic attacks or sexual struggles than we would ask a pastor to perform a root canal. Why?

Why indeed? Crabb answers his own question by pointing out that we live in a day and age where we have become conditioned to think that only highly trained professionals can meet our psychological needs, just as highly trained physicians minister to our physical ailments. But if more churches were led by godly elders who were slowly mastering the art of hard-minded but soft-hearted servanthood, then more of us would call our elders first when a problem arises. Instead, we are often led by overworked pastors slugging it out on their own, or by elders who are businessmen first and who run the church as they would a corporation.

I have thought about this litmus test in my own life. The greatest testimony to the hard-minded but soft-hearted shepherding I have received is that those dear men are the first I call upon when I'm in over my head. In the two most difficult years of my life, when my world was absolutely upside down and nothing seemed to go the way I had hoped, I found great solace and wise counsel by contacting ten elders in my life. They gave me hard-minded counsel, seasoned with large doses of soft-hearted grace. They are men I will call upon as often as trouble arises, as long as they're around. It is my heartfelt prayer to become just like them.

When elders serve by the Spirit, the impact they have becomes monumental. They inspire young men to "aspire to the overseeing—it is a fine work" (1 Timothy 3:1). The next generation of elders is built, and the torch is passed, until our Chief Shepherd returns and we head home.

CHAPTER FOUR

Don't Play the Numbers Game

It was the fall of 1970. I stood in a hallway connecting offices at Peninsula Bible Church in Palo Alto, California. I was in that hallway because of a management consulting assignment my company had accepted a short time before from PBC.

Dramatic changes were occurring in this modest-sized church located in the suburbs of a great university town. Hundreds of people were flocking to the services. Clearly something was happening, but no one quite knew what it was or what to do about it. The Spirit of God was moving among the hippie culture associated with San Francisco's Haight Ashbury district. These people were hungry to hear the Word of God and to learn about Jesus. But there were also many middle-aged engineers and their families—

people from all parts of the country—who were just beginning to move into the world of Silicon Valley and were looking for a church home.

The start of this influx was the New Year's Eve service at the beginning of that year. The place was packed with close to a thousand people. When the moderator invited new believers in the crowd to share their testimony, the Spirit of God took over and ran the proceedings for close to four hours. That was the beginning of Body Life services at PBC. For the next four years, every Sunday evening was jammed with people sharing the new life of Christ within them.

The change to PBC was overwhelming. The congregation went from some 600 people to over 3,000 in the span of six months. Conservative churchgoers found themselves sitting side-by-side with barefoot women wearing muumuu dresses. Many learned openness in sharing their life with others. Others learned to be hospitable. Most learned how to bear one another's burdens. And all learned biblical truth as it was taught expositorily by Ray Stedman, Dave Roper, and other gifted teachers.

With such explosive growth, PBC desperately needed help with financial accounting, with organizing a separate corporation to handle training and publishing functions, with building an addition for youth and adult ministries, and with many other issues which had not been troublesome when they were much smaller. Since it was my task to help them in these areas and make proposals to the board of elders, I was meeting that morning with one of the secretaries to get additional financial information.

As I entered the hallway I heard voices coming from behind an office door that was slightly ajar. The men in that office were studying the Scriptures together. After listening for a while, several things struck me forcibly.

Although I recognized the voices of Ray Stedman and Dave Roper (the main teaching pastors), no one seemed to be acting as "the expert." Everyone seemed to be entering the discussion at the same level.

These men were honest and open about their study of the Scriptures. They rarely cited theologians or well-known commentaries—they simply let God's Word speak for itself. Theological dogma and Christian cliches were absent.

These men were intensely practical in applying the Word to their own lives. There was a transparency about them as they acknowledged what God was saying through His Word to them personally.

Finally, there was a depth of reasoning and study that I had never heard before. Gone were the shallow observations I was familiar with from past men's Bible studies. These men were serious about understanding the Scriptures.

After some time, I knocked on the door and stuck my head into the room. "May I sit in for the rest of this?" I asked. "I promise not to say a word." "Of course," Stedman said (it was his office).

For the next nine months I never missed a Wednesday morning study. I even changed my travel plans because I realized this study was like gold nuggets to an out-of-work prospector. It changed my life. And it was not just studying the Scriptures with these men that so powerfully affected me, it was watching how they related to each other and carried out their ministries.

It wasn't that I was unacquainted with the Scriptures. I gave my heart to the Lord when I was six years old. I grew up in a conservative church denomination where my parents were missionaries and denominational leaders. I learned early that I had some facility for teaching the Scripture.

So what was so different about these guys? It wasn't just the way they studied the Word, it was how they acted toward each other. There wasn't a senior pastor in charge of everything. They seemed to act more like brothers than members of an organization.

I remember being quite puzzled during my ten-month consulting assignment. After all, I was a management consultant and was supposed to know how organizations worked. I had rattled around Christendom for quite a while. I should have known what was going on. Gradually the Lord helped me understand.

The process began by thinking about how organizations usually work. Since I was quite familiar with the business model, I began there. Below is a simple organizational chart representing a manager in that organization. Let's call him Joe Manager.

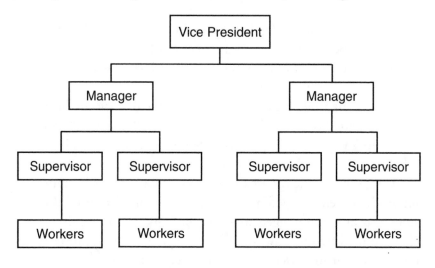

Several things are true about Joe:

• Joe's occupation identity is directly attached to his organization. The organization's goals are Joe's goals. The organization moves him around in accord with their best interests.

• Joe is placed in a *vertical* relationship. He reports to the vice-president above him and has supervisors working below him. This means Joe is in a position of *line responsibility*.

What else can be said about Joe in this organization?

- Joe's is defined by the organization as the boss (manager).
- Joe qualified for this position by competing and achieving.
- Joe's responsibility (job description) is set by the organization.
- Joe's authority comes with the position.
- Joe's evaluation is on a *quantitative* basis.

Sounds right, doesn't it? All of us have grown up learning how to fit in with a variety of organizations—schools, work at McDonald's, athletic teams, occupational jobs—which all function this way. We feel quite comfortable with this arrangement because we all know that authority doesn't come without responsibility and vice versa. Additionally, job descriptions and evaluations are quantitatively oriented. We are somewhat protected from arbitrary evaluation. Since we are not easily attacked personally, our superiors have to show we didn't carry out our responsibility before they can fire us.

The previous description is similar to the responsibility and authority structure of many Christian organizations. If we simply change the names in the boxes we have a typical church hierarchy.

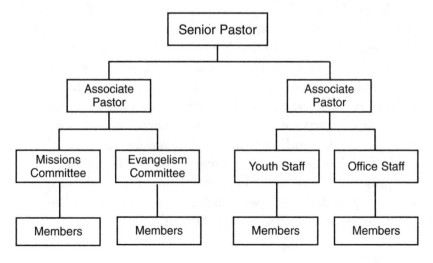

We can make exactly the same statements about the people in the Christian organization that we did about Joe in the secular organization.

- The senior pastor is defined by the church as the one in charge and the associate pastors have specific areas of responsibility under him.

- Pastors qualify for their jobs by obtaining higher education and by competing with fellow seminary graduates.

- All pastors, committees, and staff have job descriptions set by the organization of the church.

- Each pastor's authority is derived from the position.

- Each pastor's evaluation has significant *quantitative* criteria. (Notice, since the first four criteria are true, the evaluation must necessarily be quantitative.)

A pastor once told me that he had recently been evaluated in his church. He said, "It was really interesting; they set five-year goals for me." When I asked him what kinds of goals were given, he responded, "I was told that in five years I had to have three hundred more young people in my ministry than I have now." "Do you think that's realistic?" I asked. "I guess it's possible if I really work hard," he replied. He went on to explain that they were going to keep track of his progress; indeed, he had to write a report every six months detailing how he was doing.

I couldn't help thinking, "I wonder what the Lord thinks of this program?" Suppose the Lord wants him to spend the next five years bringing the young people he has to maturity in Christ—in other words, to concentrate on quality not quantity.

Did Jesus ever do that? He *did*, since He spent so much time on just twelve men. In my experience, most churches and para-church organizations are like my friend's church. They are clearly committed to doing the Lord's work but are functioning very much like secular organizations.

But perhaps you say, "What's wrong with that?" Let's go to the Scripture and see what we can learn.

While looking at how Jesus developed His organization (the Kingdom), I discovered that the disciples thought along lines very similar to us regarding organizational structures. You'll recall the aspirations of James and John that we discussed in chapter one.

> **And James and John, the two sons of Zebedee, came up to Him, saying to Him, "Teacher, we want You to do for us whatever we ask of You." And He said to them, "What do you want Me to do for you?" And they said to Him, "Grant that we may sit in Your glory, one on Your right, and one on Your left."**
>
> *Mark 10:35–37*

The disciples knew from Jesus' teachings that a kingdom was coming. They were convinced that Jesus was the Messiah and King of this new kingdom. They believed it would be the long promised earthly kingdom the Old Testament prophets had predicted.

Jesus had tried to dissuade them from their hope of an earthly kingdom. But the disciples chose to ignore His statements in favor of their enthusiasm for the overthrow of the Roman oppressors. They sought the establishment of a glorious Israeli kingdom with Jesus as the reigning King and Messiah. Because they were thinking of a physical kingdom with a government administration functioning under the king, James and John missed Jesus' point entirely. So they got the idea that they had better ask the boss (Jesus) for a high position of responsibility and authority before the rest of the disciples had a chance to do the same. Matthew records that the two brothers even got their mother involved in asking Jesus for important positions for them.

How did the other disciples feel about this request? In verse 41 we read:

And hearing this, the ten began to feel indignant with James and John.

Before we think too uncharitably about James and John, we must recognize that they were acting just as people do today within a typical church. That is, they were competing with their associates to be assigned to a higher position of authority than they presently had. They wanted vice-president on the right and vice-president on the left, and they surmised that this was as high as one could go. The other disciples thought the same thing and realized that they would be reporting to James and John. That's why they were indignant.

At first, Jesus seems to go along with them. He questions them about their qualifications for the jobs they are seeking.

But Jesus said to them, "You do not know what you are asking for. Are you able to drink the cup that I drink, or to be baptized with the baptism with which I am baptized?" And they said to Him, "We are able."

Mark 10:38

Jesus is saying, "Gentlemen, there are some tough qualifications for these jobs." He uses two metaphors—the *cup* and *baptism*. He was referring to the cup of the experience that He would have to endure. The psalmists used this phrase many times in the Old Testament.

Baptism means to be submerged in something. From our perspective, we know that Jesus is talking about being submerged in the rejection, the hatred, the agony, and the death of the cross. He is asking them, "Are you able to participate in that? That is what the job calls for." They glibly reply, "You bet. We can handle it." But Jesus goes on to say that the Kingdom organization is quite different from what they suppose. He gives two clues in verse 39.

> **And Jesus said to them, "The cup that I drink you shall drink; and you shall be baptized with the baptism with which I am baptized. But to sit on My right or on My left, this is not Mine to give; but it is for those for whom it has been prepared."**

The first thing Jesus says is that leadership positions cannot be granted by either He or the organization. "I cannot grant you that position." The second thing He says is that the position is prepared for the person, not the other way around. That's quite a change from the organizations most of us are used to. I would have thought, "What do you mean, the boss, the Messiah, can't give us vice-president positions in the kingdom? I've never heard of an organization tailoring positions to fit the person. What's going on here?"

Thankfully, Jesus goes on to explain what He meant.

> **And calling them to Himself, Jesus said to them, "You know that those who are recognized as rulers of the Gentiles lord it over them; and their great men exercise authority over them. But it is not so among you, but whoever wishes to become great among you shall be your servant; and whoever wishes to be first among you shall be slave of all. For even the Son of Man did not come to be served, but to serve, and to give His life a ransom for many."**

> *Mark 10:42–45*

Do you understand what Jesus is saying? There is something about how the kingdom functions that is quite different from what we are used to. Most organizations require that authority and responsibility be exercised over others. But My kingdom doesn't work that way.

There are at least four principles comparing the differences between how Jesus wants His kingdom to function with most of the organizations we know.

1. *Brotherhood* — The line of responsibility (or chain of command) in the typical hierarchy or pyramid structure is not acceptable in Christ's Kingdom. Applied to the church this means that associate pastors should not report to "senior" pastors. You may remember that on a different occasion Jesus said, "One is your master" (meaning Jesus) and you are all brothers (all on the same level).

2. *Servant-leadership* — Greatness in leadership does not proceed from appointments made by the organization, but from servant-hood. One has to learn to serve others. This fits with what Jesus told James and John: "Any position in my kingdom is prepared for the person."

3. *Bondservanthood* — The criterion (job description) for leader-ship in the kingdom requires being a bondservant. A bondservant in Jesus' day was someone who chose to be a servant for life, doing his master's will. Furthermore, it involves a willingness to be last instead of first.

4. *Giving up rights* — Jesus Christ, as a bondservant, is our leader-ship model. He gave up all His rights—everything He had—to serve others. Therefore it seems that the church must be organized quite differently than most organizations. In other words, we should not take secular management and organizational principles and apply them to the church if we want to be serious about what Jesus says.

What can we do then? We must revamp our picture of the leadership model.

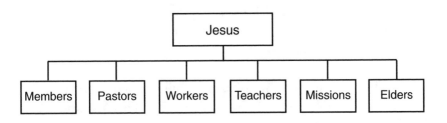

Here we have a horizontal structure in contrast to a pyramid. Jesus is the head; everyone reports directly to Him. Yet they are all on the same level with each other. This eliminates line responsibility, thus fulfilling Jesus' statement, "Their great men exercise authority over them. But it is not so among you." No one is in authority over anyone else.

This does not mean there are no leaders—there *are*. But these leaders are not "over" someone; they are not "lording it over others" because they have positions of responsibility. Rather, these leaders serve from *underneath*. This is a radical concept, but it is entirely scriptural.

In this scenario what are the specific characteristics of the leader?

- First, the leader is recognized by the Body of Christ, not by an organization. That is, ordinary people in the local church identify their own leaders on the basis of service. This is what happened in Acts 6:3 when the congregation put forward seven men to help provide for widows. These men were already known to be full of the Holy Spirit and to be servants of the Body.

- Second, the leader is qualified on the basis of spiritual gifts and faith. There is no competition because the Holy Spirit assigns the particular leadership gifts "just as He wills" (1 Corinthians 12:11), and people in the Body see these gifts being exercised by faith.

- Third, the leader's area of responsibility is defined by the Lord as explained in 1 Corinthians 12:5. Thus the leader naturally moves to serve in a particular area of need.

- Fourth, the leader's authority comes from the Body because the people who are being ministered to willingly choose to submit to the leader. The Spirit from within the people authenticates the actual servant-leading of their leader. No title or position causes this response.

- Finally, the leader's evaluation is *qualitative,* not quantitative. Galatians 5:22–23 lists the fruit of the Spirit. Notice that these all relate to who a person is, not what he does. Can quantitative criteria be placed on the fruit of the Spirit? No—these are clearly concerned with quality. This is why the numbers game does not work with leaders in the Kingdom. Nor should it work, because God might "assign" a faithful leader to a ministry where ten years of work produces one convert. Is this quantity acceptable by God's standards? It can be. How can anyone of us guess what God is going to do when He is maturing men and women in Jesus Christ and building into them the qualities of the Holy Spirit? How can anyone put a quantitative value on that?

You may now be wondering, "How does leadership apply to elders?" "How should they oversee the church?" Read on—the leadership characteristics described in this chapter will be applied to elders in Part Two.

CHAPTER FIVE

Elders or Deacons:
What's the Difference?

What was the first crisis in the leadership and administration of the New Testament church? It was not the persecution of Peter and John, nor was it the revelation of Ananias and Sapphira's deceit. It occurred when the administrative burden of the growing Body became too much for the apostles/elders to handle.

The fledgling church responded to the crisis by selecting the first seven deacons. Every elder who has ever served in the local church knows that this crisis repeats itself in every church. How do we distinguish between the roles of elders and deacons? How do we keep those functions distinct when we ought to and combine them when appropriate?

Nothing is more frustrating for a group of elders than getting bogged down by the administrative work that is rightfully the duty of deacons—especially since elders and deacons have each received a separate calling and gifting from God.

For an elder, discerning the functional differences between elders and deacons is an essential skill. It's easy to be confused about the distinction.

The Scriptures, however, reveal to us that a clear distinction exists. In Acts chapter 20 the apostle Paul addressed the Ephesian elders, bidding them farewell as he was on his way to Jerusalem (Acts 20:17–38). Here we see three different terms that refer to elders. They are *elders* (v. 17), *overseers* ("bishops" KJV, v. 28), and *shepherd* (verb form, v. 28).

These three terms are used interchangeably to refer to the same men. They are applied to those who are to "keep watch over . . . all the flock" (v. 28). In other words, "elders" and "overseers" are to do the work of "pastors" (or "shepherds"), which is to "shepherd the flock."

The term *elder* emphasizes the spiritual maturity and experience of one who shepherds—that is who he is. The term *overseer* emphasizes the man's functional responsibility—that is what he does. And the term *shepherd* more specifically describes his ministry—to heed, lead, and feed the local flock.

In terms of specific ministry, the Scripture has much to say regarding *elders* (i.e., bishops, overseers, and pastors/shepherds). Elders are responsible to oversee and lead the local congregation (Acts 20:28; 1 Timothy 3:1–2; Titus 1:5, 7). They are to preach and teach in the local church (1 Timothy 5:17; Hebrews 13:7). They are to exhort the church in sound doctrine and refute those who contradict them (Titus 1:9), and assist those who are spiritually weak (1 Thessalonians 5:12–14). Lastly, they are to care for and shepherd the flock (Acts 20:28; 1 Peter 5:1–2; Hebrews 13:17).

But what about the deacons? The term *deacon* simply means "one who serves." Originally, it referred to one who waited on tables. This is why many believe that the first deacons seen in the New Testament are those seven men who were chosen to meet the needs of the Grecian widows in Acts 6:1–6.

The word *deacon* came to denote any service done in the local church. In an official sense, however, deacons serve under the leadership and oversight of the elders (1 Timothy 3:8–13). They assist the elders in exercising the oversight in the practical matters of church life.

In contrast to the specific responsibilities that Scripture gives to elders, the Bible nowhere defines official or specific responsibilities for deacons. Rather, such responsibilities seem to be left up to the elders to assign to deacons as the needs arise.

It should be noted that many biblical churches do not claim to have elders at all. Instead, they have what they call *deacons* or *trustees* who perform the duties we attribute to elders.

Your church may have strong reasons for retaining the current titles for their church leaders, particularly if your denominational tradition calls these men by another name. However, we recommend that each church examine carefully who is fulfilling the role of elder as defined in this book. It is critical to ensure that a distinct and separate group of leaders is attending to the duties described in Acts 6:1–6. Keep in mind that our primary concern is not with the names you may ascribe to your elders, but rather that biblical servant/ leadership is practiced by those leaders as they follow Christ.

Some Diagnostics

Here is a diagnostic test to help you discern what is properly the role of the deacon, and what duties should belong to the elder. There are twenty-five questions. On the left side of the page is a list of tasks or decisions facing a local church. On the right side is a column titled "Elder's Role" and another, "Deacon's Role." If you think the task or decision lies with the elders, put a check in the elder's column. If you think the task or decision lies with those gifted for a deacon's ministry, put a check in the deacon's column. At the end of the chapter, we will answer each question, and give you our reasons for choosing the way we did. Our answers appear on pages 88 to 93.

Churches might prayerfully consider having all their elders and deacons take this same test. It could be interesting and revealing to see what kind of dialogue this test sparks at the next elder meeting.

TASK/DECISION	ELDER'S ROLE	DEACON'S ROLE
Determine the annual preaching schedule		
Contact every family in the church by phone		
Interview and hire a new youth pastor		
Hire a new gardener		
Confront a man who is cheating on his wife		
Order new hymnbooks		
Develop a policy for designated giving		
Put together a team to produce a church newsletter		
Bring meals and tapes to shut-ins		
Develop a vision and mission statement for the church		

TASK/DECISION	ELDER'S ROLE	DEACON'S ROLE
Set aside a season of prayer for the Body		
Disciple young men in the Body/train leaders		
Repave the parking lot		
Agree to support a missionary to unreached peoples		
Organize a prayer chain		
Read and respond to letters from the congregation		
Upgrade the sound system		
Oversee the team of volunteers for Vacation Bible School		
Rent and drive vans for the student mission trip		
Greet worshipers at the door each Sunday		
Turn off the A/C and lock up after Sunday evening		
Organize the annual baptism/ communion services		
Compose or revise the doctrinal statement		
Write and produce the weekly bulletin		
Respond to a visiting speaker who teaches error		

It is sometimes difficult to know for sure which answer is right, or if a third column entitled "Pastor" should be added, or even if a possible fourth column entitled "All." Certainly, godly men may differ in their judgement.

So, how do we discern a clearly marked path for elders? How do elders serve faithfully without getting bogged down with minutiae?

The Service of Elders, In Order of Priority

Serving by Praying

This is related to our chapter on the crucial importance of listening to God through prayer. Simply put, praying and listening to God to discern the mind of Christ in unanimity is the first service to which elders are called. The original twelve apostles in Jerusalem made this perfectly clear in Acts 6:2–4:

> **And the twelve summoned the congregation of the disciples and said, "It is not desirable for us to neglect the word of God in order to serve tables. But select from among you, brethren, seven men of good reputation, full of the Spirit and of wisdom, whom we may put in charge of this task. But we will devote ourselves to prayer, and to the ministry of the word."**

This is the first word from these early church leaders concerning the number one priority of all elders—to devote themselves to prayer.

One word must be highlighted here: *devote*. We all know the strangling feeling that comes when the "to do" list keeps growing, the daylight hours keep shrinking, and the displeasure and grumbling of the congregation is sorely felt. We tend to abandon our devotion to prayer and throw ourselves into the work even more vigorously.

But elders are not called to be firemen, nor are they called to jump whenever the congregation says to. Rather, elders are to devote themselves consistently to prayer for the benefit and blessing of the Body.

A word of warning: No work in the church is more important for elders than praying, yet no work is more difficult when it comes to practice and devotion. There are a million distractions hurled at us like gunfire, and the temptation is always to reach for something we can do rather than getting on our knees. We all know that it is a good thing to pray; in fact, it is the first and best thing an elder can do. But when the pressure rises, it is easy to forget that the most effective way an elder serves is by praying.

James 5:13–18 has a specific application of this when the elders are called on to pray for the sick in the local assembly. It is intriguing that James exhorts the elders to pray, illustrating his thought by reminding them of the prayers of Elijah during the days of the drought in ancient Israel under King Ahab. Remember Elijah's prayer. He prayed seven times for the rain to return. Elijah was a human being just like any elder in the local church. But he was a man of consistent, faithful prayer.

Such is the prayer life to which an elder is called, not just a one-time quickie prayer when the sick are anointed and the elders are called upon to pray publicly. Elijah prayed with fervency and consistency—and so should all elders!

Paul the Apostle is also a wonderful example of the praying elder. One cannot read far in most of his epistles without realizing that Paul prayed constantly for the churches he addressed. (See Romans 1:9–10; 1 Corinthians 1:4; Ephesians 1:15–23; Philippians 1:3–5; Colossians 1:3–8; 1 Thessalonians 1:2–5; and 2 Thessalonians 1:11–12). Paul prayed for these churches "always." So should all elders.

Serving by Feeding the Sheep

If we take the priorities of the apostles in Acts 6, we see that elders are next called to devote themselves "to the service of the Word"—the preaching and teaching of the biblical text. The apostles knew that the first need of the fledgling church was to be fed with the Word of God. They actively chose not to be distracted from that crucial service to the Body.

Moreover, Jesus Himself commissioned Peter as the first elder with the thrice-repeated command to feed and tend the sheep. In the mind of Christ, the Good Shepherd, a crucial task of the elder is to feed the sheep. While this may mean that the elders serve as the primary preachers and teachers within the local Body, it does not imply that the elders alone should be teaching and preaching. They should also look to encourage the teaching ministry of the "not yet" elders and visiting teachers who may have fresh insights to contribute to the local Body. Overall, elders are to ensure that the Body has a balanced diet of solid biblical exposition, from the pulpit to the classroom, from the preschool class to the most mature saints.

We recall the installation service of one elder in our church. This man was a doctor who served the poor in our city by giving them free medical care. He had also served in a Southern Baptist hospital in a militantly Muslim country. He was a seasoned and gracious gentleman. One of the brothers asked him how the Body could pray for him. His response was profound. He said simply, "Please pray that I will know what it means to feed the sheep."

Serving by Compassionately Walking Among the Sheep

In Acts 20:17–38, Paul wrote a veritable handbook on how elders are to serve. The first thing he calls to their minds is this—Paul had served the flock simply by being with them. He walked among them day and night, and he was not distracted by divergent ministries that would take him from his primary task. He knew those sheep.

Paul describes his service among them: ". . . remembering that night and day for a period of three years I did not cease to admonish each one with tears." Twice Paul speaks of the tears with which he served the Ephesian church (Acts 20:19, 31). He cared so deeply for the sheep that he wept over them.

Paul was instructing the elders of the Ephesian church how to shepherd the flock. His emphasis addressed two primary areas: feeding the sheep by teaching "the whole counsel of God" (Acts 20:27), and walking compassionately among the sheep (Acts 20:18–21, 31). It is only when elders grow distant to the sheep that they become hardened to their needs, becoming like the false shepherds of Israel identified by Ezekiel.

> Woe, shepherds of Israel who have been feeding themselves! Should not the shepherds feed the flock? You eat the fat and clothe yourselves with the wool, you slaughter the fat sheep without feeding the flock. Those who are sickly you have not strengthened, the diseased you have not healed, the broken you have not bound up, the scattered you have not brought back, nor have you sought for the lost; but with force and with severity you have dominated them.
>
> *Ezekiel 34:2–4*

What a contrast to the compassionate Paul!

Serving by Guarding the Doctrine

While elders are to be compassionate toward the sheep, they are to be stern when dealing with false teachers who would steal the sheep away. Paul warns the Ephesian elders about this crucial task in Acts 20:28–30:

> Be on guard for yourselves and for all the flock, among which the Holy Spirit has made you overseers,

to shepherd the church of God which He purchased with His own blood. I know that after my departure savage wolves will come in among you, not sparing the flock; and from among your own selves men will arise, speaking perverse things, to draw away the disciples after them.

Paul also instructed Titus to ensure that the men whom he appointed as elders on the island of Crete were astute in knowing and guarding the doctrine. Paul told Titus that each of these men must be "holding fast the faithful word which is in accordance with the teaching, that he may be able both to exhort in sound doctrine and to refute those who contradict" (Titus 1:9).

For several years, a group of men had been leading an intern program in their church. These men were gradually developing a unique theology of their own and passing that theology on to the impressionable young interns. None of the elders knew this was happening until the Lord suddenly started to decrease the giving for a season. That got the elders' attention!

As the finances plummeted, the elders began to pray about what was happening in the church. The Lord began to direct them to ask questions about what was happening with the intern program. The questionable theology was identified and the teachers were graciously approached and reasoned with. Some months later it became clear that the intern teachers needed to pursue their alternate theology in an alternate setting.

Imagine for a moment that the elders had not been grounded in the Scriptures. Suppose they had to go "toe-to-toe" with these theological thinkers who did nothing but study every day. Who would win the debate? The entire situation might have ended very differently had these elders not possessed a firm understanding of Scripture. It is imperative for elders to know the truth so well that it will not prove difficult to identify and remove the counterfeit.

Serving by Leading

Perhaps the greatest complaint against elder-led churches is that there is precious little leadership exerted. Elders must realize that the people perish without a vision. It is critical for the sheep to have confidence that the elders are leading them diligently. Peter throws great light on this subject in his exhortation to elders:

> **Therefore, I exhort the elders among you, as your fellow elder and witness of the sufferings of Christ, and a partaker also of the glory that is to be revealed, shepherd the flock of God among you, exercising oversight not under compulsion, but voluntarily, according to the will of God; and not for sordid gain, but with eagerness; nor yet as lording it over those allotted to your charge, but proving to be examples to the flock. And when the Chief Shepherd appears, you will receive the unfading crown of glory.**
>
> *1 Peter 5:1–4*

Clearly, Peter is envisioning the elder as an eager leader, faithfully and actively shepherding the sheep while leading as their moral and spiritual example. The elder is not whipping them by lording authority over them, but leading by virtue of being a good shepherd. If the saying "leaders must lead" is true, then the phrase "elders must lead" is also true, with this added stipulation: "elders must lead—by praying and responding to Christ as He leads."

But this leadership is hard work. It is leadership on its knees—listening, seeking to know and the mind and will of Christ, and not making hasty decisions. To fail to do the hard work of praying and listening, to fail to come to unanimity and make definite decisions, is to abrogate the God-given leadership to which elders are called.

In summary, these five means of serving define the biblical role of an elder:

- seeking the mind of Christ by praying
- seeking the mind of Christ in knowing how to feed the sheep
- seeking the mind of Christ in how to walk compassionately among the sheep
- seeking the mind of Christ in guarding the doctrine
- seeking the mind of Christ to see where He is leading.

Much of the "ministrivia" in which elders find themselves engaged may not fit within these categories. We may be tempted to lump all the minutiae of ministry under the leadership umbrella, but that is illogical. The leader who is bogged down by administrative detail is not even able to see where he is, much less where he is going.

What then is the function of a New Testament deacon? First, it is practical service—serving the needs of the members of the Body, such as providing food and administering specific physical aid to the needy in the Body (as in Acts 6). Elders are shepherds who discern the mind of Christ—it is spiritually strategic in nature. Deacons are servants who are involved in becoming the hands of Christ—it is practical and tactical in nature.

Now that we have a better framework for distinguishing between elders and deacons, let's revisit our diagnostic test, but with some answers and discussion.

Some Diagnostics—Revisited

TASK/DECISION	ELDER'S ROLE	DEACON'S ROLE
Determine the annual preaching schedule	X	

One of the primary ways elders serve is by "feeding the sheep." A crucial aspect of this is overseeing the pulpit ministry.

TASK/DECISION	ELDER'S ROLE	DEACON'S ROLE
Contact every family in the church by phone	X	

A great way to "walk compassionately with the sheep," as is leading home fellowship groups. Yet deacons may also do this.

Interview and hire a new youth pastor	X	

This falls under "feeding the sheep" and "leading." Selecting a new youth pastor is a crucial responsibility of elders.

Hire a new gardener		X

Ensuring that the physical plant and property are well-maintained is a practical ministry for the deacons.

Confront a man who is cheating on his wife	X	

This falls under the category of "walking compassionately among the sheep."

Order new hymnbooks	X	X

Primarily a physical service to the Body. But elders may wish to review different hymnbooks for spiritual content and effectiveness in leading the Body to worship, then pass the baton to the deacons to order the books and place them in the pews.

TASK/DECISION	ELDER'S ROLE	DEACON'S ROLE
Develop a policy for designated giving	X	

Elders must lead the Body in the legal and godly ways of giving to specific needs.

Put together a team to produce a church newsletter	X	

A means of communicating to the Body and enriching them spiritually. The key is delegation: elders assemble a team to produce the newsletter, then trust them to get it done.

Bring meals and tapes to shut-ins		X

A classic function of deacons, reflecting the heart of Acts 6.

Develop a vision and mission statement for the church	X	

A function of the elders, falling under the category of "leading."

Set aside a season of prayer for the Body	X	

When the Body faces a crucial juncture, elders may establish a time of prayer to learn what the Lord is doing.

Disciple young men in the Body/train leaders	X	

A crucial responsibility for elders, "feeding" and "leading" the sheep.

TASK/DECISION	ELDER'S ROLE	DEACON'S ROLE
Repave the parking lot		X
This is a very practical, hands-on ministry for deacons.		
Agree to support a missionary to unreached peoples	X	
"Feeding the sheep" via a teaching ministry to future sheep. Elders must discern the giftedness and maturity of candidates.		
Organize a prayer chain		X
Compiling lists and numbers and identifying prayer-chain captains is a deacon ministry.		
Read and respond to letters from the congregation	X	
Shepherding by the elders as they walk compassionately among the sheep. They must consider the letters before the Lord, and respond.		
Upgrade the sound system		X
The deacons serve by providing equipment so that everyone in the auditorium can hear. In a sense, this is serving spiritual "food" to the Body.		
Oversee the team of volunteers for Vacation Bible School	X	
A task of the elders, as they "walk compassionately among the sheep."		

Task/Decision	Elder's Role	Deacon's Role
Rent and drive vans for the student mission trip		X
A practical ministry that should be supervised by the deacons.		
Greet worshipers at the door each Sunday	X	
Elders express the welcoming love of Christ to the Body. "Walking compassionately among the sheep."		
Turn off the A/C and lock up after Sunday evening		X
Maintaining the facilities and property by exercising good stewardship is a ministry and responsibility of the deacons.		
Organize the baptism/ communion services	X	
Elders must ensure that the ordinances given to the church by Jesus are recognized and obeyed. This is "leading" by setting an example of obedience.		
Compose or revise the doctrinal statement	X	
Overseeing and guarding flock belongs to the elders. Falls under "guarding the doctrine."		

TASK/DECISION	ELDER'S ROLE	DEACON'S ROLE
Write and produce the bulletin	X	X

A tough call. The bulletin is communication with the church Body. The information conveyed is *primarily* the responsibility of the elders. The weekly composition, printing, and folding of the bulletin is the responsibility of the deacons.

TASK/DECISION	ELDER'S ROLE	DEACON'S ROLE
Respond to a visiting speaker who teaches error	X	

An important function of the elders, falling under the category "guarding the doctrine."

A Final Thought

So, how can we encourage the ministry of deacons in our churches? Here is one recommendation: a network of home fellowship groups where a small number of gifted believers are encouraged to serve one another and meet the practical needs of brothers and sisters within the home fellowship group.

This behind-the-scenes service by the deacons can provide a loving context of ongoing relationship and community, thereby strengthening the service of the deacons. Such service may evolve as an "independent contractor" type of ministry, led by the Spirit, enabling deacons and deaconesses to respond quickly to the needs of the Body.

Scripturally, we have record of deacons being selected in the Jerusalem church only, though qualifications for deacons are listed in 1 Timothy 3. Once they were selected, they probably served individually. There is no further reference to a group of deacons in

Scripture. Titus was not charged to appoint deacons in every city, although he was to appoint elders.

While there is no further record of a collective meeting of deacons, there is the dramatic record of the collective meeting of elders at the Jerusalem Council in Acts 15. It is likely that deacons and deaconesses served in a network of home-fellowships, under the leadership of the Spirit. This harmonizes with the scriptural account.

Elders serve by discerning what the tasks and decisions of elders and deacons look like. Elders should not find themselves distracted by or buried under tasks that others in the Body have been gifted and set apart to do. May God grant us wisdom and discernment in these areas so that elders may be free to lead spiritually, and deacons may be free to serve the practical needs of the Body.

CHAPTER SIX

What Elders Need To Know: A Biblical Framework

We have discussed many specific aspects of New Testament leadership by elders, and how our Lord has led various elders to tackle a number of different issues and challenges. But how does all this really work for you in your church?

In this chapter we will discuss the framework of biblical truth undergirding all that we have written about. As a Body has a skeleton of bones, and a building has its structural supports, so an elder must have a spiritual framework of truth from the Scripture upholding his every thought, prayer, and decision.

If a group of elders doesn't have this framework, their church will be little more than a house of cards, just waiting to be blown down by a problem their framework can't handle. I've seen one elder-led church forced to shut its doors because the elders just didn't have this spiritual framework in place.

I recall attending an elder retreat one weekend in the California Sierras. Every January this group of elders would go away to review the past year and envision the year ahead. This was my first retreat, and I was fascinated to see what God would do. Getting away together to seek the mind of Christ in a quiet place far from the trenches and the unremitting problems of daily church life is essential. What would God show these men?

Our discussion was guided by two questions: First, what do most American Christians encounter when they walk through the door of a church? And second, what do we desire our sheep to encounter when they walk through the doors of our church?

These were good questions, and there were stimulating answers all around. In response to the first question, most of the men thought that many American Christians were sitting under light-weight teaching, and that far too many churches spent too much effort trying to entertain their people. Others thought there was too little emphasis on real worship in our "worship" services, and that far too often Sunday morning services distracted them from intimacy with Christ. Another man cited the dearth of real ministries of compassion in the modern church.

But when we addressed the second question, things came sharply into focus. Each man shared a vision the Lord had put on his heart. It was usually a direct reflection of each man's primary spiritual gifts. Our administrative elder wanted to see a church where every program was well-run and where the needs of the churchgoer were diligently thought through beforehand. He wanted the church to be a smooth-running operation. Our man with a mercy gift spoke of ministries to the poor in the city, where folks could come to church and find access to practical ministries of compassion in our town.

When it came to me, I shared this vision: "My dream is to have our people come through the doors and encounter the living Christ—Christ residing in His people who are using their spiritual gifts, hearing from Him when He speaks through the preaching and teaching of the Word, demonstrated in His Body as everyone serves Him and one another. My desire is for them to know the heart of the gospel: 'Christ in you, the hope of glory' (Colossians 1:27). It is what the Christian life is when He lives His resurrection life in and through us. That is my dream."

One of the men looked at me dumbfounded and said, "What? I have no idea what you are talking about." And he was dead right! He had no clue. His ministry was bereft of spiritual fruit. He had worked himself to the point of burnout. He was looking to cut back his involvement in the church as soon as possible.

This brother was an intelligent man. His problem was that he had no spiritual framework for understanding how God equips His chosen elders to conduct the weighty ministry to which they are called. In the end, it seemed that he was operating almost exclusively by his flesh. He appeared to be smart, but he was actually cold and calculating. He did everything by the numbers. And when the numbers declared him a failure, he wanted out.

His ministry as an elder—and that church—were both a house of cards. Neither one had a real framework. They were destined to be blown down by the hellish winds of opposition from the evil one.

No one wants to be there. We all want a strong framework to withstand the storms that inevitably come our way. But what is that framework?

The Backbone: The "Christ In You" Life

The most important concept for Christians to understand is the essence of "Christ in you, the hope of glory"—the eternal life we enjoy in Christ (Colossians 1:27). It is important for all Christians, but doubly important for elders to know what the "Christ in you" life is, and to live and think accordingly. So what is the "Christ in you" life?

This radical idea that God would come to live in any man, woman, boy, or girl who believed in Him was outlined in Ezekiel 36:26–28. That passage refers to the days in which we now live when the Holy Spirit indwells all believers:

> **Moreover, I will give you a new heart and put a new spirit within you; and I will remove the heart of stone from your flesh and give you a heart of flesh. And I will put My Spirit within you and cause you to walk in My statutes, and you will be careful to observe My ordinances. And you will live in the land that I gave to your forefathers; so you will be My people, and I will be your God.**

Jesus Himself gave us the ordinance of communion, or the Lord's Supper, not only to picture His redemptive work on Calvary, but also to illustrate the reality of His indwelling presence in our lives by faith in Him (Mark 14:22–24; 1 Corinthians 11:17–34). The practice of the Lord's Supper illustrates the spiritual reality of Christ in you, dramatized in physical terms that we aren't likely to forget.

The sacrament pictures Jesus Christ, "the bread of life" (John 6:48), coming to live within us. Spiritually, we "eat His body and drink His blood" (See John 6:47–56) in the sense that by faith we partake of His Person and life. Partaking of Christ is necessary for our spiritual sustenance—for our spiritual and eternal life. We are to do this "in remembrance of Him," not as a historical remembrance, but to remember He is alive, right now, living inside us.

Jesus gave us a marvelous illustration of this in John 15:5:

> I am the vine, you are the branches; he who
> abides in Me, and I in him, he bears much fruit;
> for apart from Me you can do nothing.

Paul translates all this theology in a few concise verses, starting in Romans 2: 28–29 with the radical change in a Christian:

> For he is not a Jew who is one outwardly; nei-
> ther is circumcision that which is outward in
> the flesh; but he is a Jew who is one inwardly;
> and circumcision is that which is of the heart,
> by the Spirit, not by the letter; and his praise is
> not from men, but from God.

Paul carries this idea further in 2 Corinthians 3:5–6, describing the life within us by the Spirit:

> Not that we are adequate in ourselves to con-
> sider anything as coming from ourselves, but
> our adequacy is from God, who also made us
> adequate as servants of a new covenant, not of
> the letter, but of the Spirit; for the letter kills,
> but the Spirit gives life.

Then Paul stated this even more succinctly in Colossians 1:27—indeed this may be the theme verse of the New Testament:

> . . . to whom God willed to make known what is
> the riches of the glory of this mystery among the
> Gentiles, which is Christ in you, the hope of
> glory.

This is the heart of the great news about Christ: that Christ lives inside believers by the Holy Spirit, changing their hearts, relating to them intimately, and empowering them to be adequate for their calling.

This is the backbone of an elder's framework for effective shepherding. Without it he is paralyzed. To gain a more complete understanding of the "Christ in you" life, one needs to study Romans 1 through 8, observing how Paul used the first seven chapters to point toward chapter eight, where he unveiled the secret of the indwelling Spirit. The Spirit defines the Christian (8:9), enables the Christian to relate to God as an adopted son (8:14–16), and empowers the Christian to have victory over sin and endure suffering with great hope (8:11–13; 8:17–26). Furthermore, 2 Corinthians 2–4 outlines where the adequacy of the Christian lies—with the indwelling Holy Spirit alone.

To expand our understanding of the "Christ in you" life, let me quote extensively from a man to whom I owe an immeasurable debt. It was from his lips that I first learned this great truth. Here is Major Ian Thomas's summary on the last two pages of *The Saving Life of Christ:*

> *The Lord Jesus Christ claims the use of your body, your whole being, your complete personality, so that as you give yourself to Him through the eternal Spirit, He may give Himself to you through the eternal Spirit, that all your activity as a human being on earth may be His activity in and through you; that every step you take, every word you speak, everything you do, everything you are, may be an expression of the Son of God, in you as man.*

> *If it is of Him and through Him and to Him, where do you come in? You do not! That is just where you go out! That is what Paul meant when he said, "For me to live is Christ"*

(Philippians 1:21). The only Person whom God credits with the right to live in you is Jesus Christ; so reckon yourself to be dead to all that you are apart from what He is, and alive unto God only in all that you are because of what He is (Romans 6:11).

When the world looked at Jesus Christ, they saw God! They heard Him speak and they saw Him act. And Jesus said, "As My Father hath sent me, even so I send you" (John 20:21). The world again will hear God speak and see God act!

It is for you to BE—it is for Him to DO! Restfully available to the Saving Life of Christ, enjoying "the richest measure of the divine Presence, a body wholly filled and flooded with God Himself," instantly obedient to the heavenly impulse—this is your vocation, and this is your victory! [Thomas's emphasis.]

This "Christ in you" life is the backbone of eldering. It is Christ inside the elder, leading His church through that man's singular decision, which Christ will bring to unanimity with His other elders. In this way, the elders incarnate the mind of Christ in practical decision-making, allowing the living Christ to lead His church in its daily activities.

Spiritual Gifts

Another essential part of the framework of biblical eldering is a clear understanding of spiritual gifts. We have spoken of the importance of spiritual gifts—the gifts the elders possess—and how critical it is for elders to be hard-minded but soft-hearted when evaluating the spiritual gifts of other believers and leaders within the Body. But what are spiritual gifts?

Spiritual gifts are supernatural capacities that enable us to express the life of Christ to a broken world. They produce His character within those whom He redeems. They are spiritual capacities given by God, enabling believers to serve others in order to build up the Body of Christ into spiritual maturity.

Elders must be able to distinguish between spiritual gifts and natural talents. Natural talents are abilities a person is born with, and they are abilities that can be developed over time. By contrast, a spiritual gift is a supernatural capacity placed within the believer by the Holy Spirit. It too can be trained and developed, but it is supernatural—part of deity clothed in humanity.

This particular distinction was brought home to a friend of mine one day while he was driving in his car. On the radio Frank Sinatra was singing one of my friend's favorite hymns. The song was "The Old Rugged Cross." It was the first time my friend had ever heard Sinatra sing a hymn.

As he listened, he thought to himself "That's really nice. What a great voice!" But only a few minutes later, as he was changing stations, my friend heard something that made his senses tingle. George Beverly Shea was singing "The Old Rugged Cross." At once, the difference between natural talent and a spiritual gift came crashing home to my friend. He found his heart ministered to in a supernatural way because of Shea's gift of encouragement. Sinatra's rendition appealed to the ear, but it didn't touch the soul.

To help us between natural talents and spiritual gifts, we turn to four passages in the New Testament: Ephesians 4:1–16, 1 Peter 4:7–11, Romans 12:1–8, and 1 Corinthians 12–14. Twenty-one gifts are listed in these passages.

Offices: Ephesians 4:11

Apostle — One who was specifically sent from God, as His representative, for a specific purpose. There are no more apostles today (or prophets), since the ministry of the apostles and prophets was for the purpose of establishing the "foundation" of the New Testament Church (Ephesians 2:20 cf. Matthew 16:18). When you build a building, you only build the foundation once.

Prophet — The prophet spoke the words of God, revealing the heart of God with regard to the specific situation of His people. The prophet was God's mouthpiece to the people before the written message was completed. Thus, the office of prophet is no longer operative today since the Old Testament and New Testament writings are complete, although the gift of prophecy (preaching) is still operative.

Evangelist — A messenger of good news. In the context of the gospel, or the good news, the evangelist is the proclaimer of that good news. This is a supernatural capacity to proclaim the truth of the gospel to nonbelievers with great effect and fruitfulness.

Pastor-Teacher — One who guides, directs, and protects the sheep, and feeds them via the systematic teaching of the Word of God. Such teaching will be most effective if it is clear, accurate, and expository.

Speaking Gifts: 1 Peter 4:7–11, Romans 12:1–8, and 1 Corinthians 12–14

Prophecy — The ability to speak forth the Word of God, causing it to illumine people in a compelling manner. A gifted preacher, whose piercing and relevant messages illuminate the Scriptures in fresh ways, exercises this gift.

Teaching — The ability to teach the Bible, providing believers with sound instruction in biblical doctrine.

Wisdom — The ability to exercise good judgment in the face of the demands of life, based on scriptural insight.

Knowledge — The ability to come to a broad knowledge of the revelation of God in His Word, and to order and systematize that knowledge in a clear fashion. The ability to unravel the mysteries of God to the degree they are revealed in the Bible.

Exhortation/Encouragement — The ability to come alongside a fellow believer to encourage, comfort, challenge, exhort, or otherwise befriend them for the purpose of helping them grow.

Discernment — The ability to distinguish between good and evil, between what is of the Spirit of God and what is of different spirits.

Leadership — The ability to stand before and lead people with care and effectiveness, having vision for what God wants done.

Tongues — The ability to speak a known human language previously unknown to the person as a means of praising God. It is also a sign to Jewish unbelievers. This gift requires interpretation to be of full value in corporate worship.

Interpretation of Tongues — The ability to interpret the outward expression of the gift of tongues, making the message understandable to others.

Miracles — The ability to perform mighty acts of supernatural power as an attestation to the power inherent in the gospel of Jesus Christ.

Serving Gifts: 1 Peter 4:7–11, Romans 12:1–8, and 1 Corinthians 12–14

Administration — The ability to do all the practical steps needed for the "ship of ministry" to sail smoothly and easily. The one with this gift masters the details and is a coordinator, making sure nothing slips through the cracks.

Faith — The ability to pray with great confidence, or the person who has a clear vision for how a ministry should function and fully expects God to carry out the vision.

Mercy — The ability to show active pity or compassion for one who is in need physically, emotionally, or spiritually, or who is in helpless distress.

Helps — The ability to provide physical aid and assistance, usually with little or no direct contact with people. This is a ministry of taking care of "things" that need doing, either in personal lives or in a ministry setting.

Service — The ability to serve people in order to aid and support them physically or personally, making them sense God's care for their physical or personal needs.

Giving — The ability to give liberally from one's financial or other personal resources, as God specifically directs, to those in need or to those serving in ministry.

Healing — The ability to heal someone physically, emotionally, or spiritually.

Understanding our own spiritual gifts and wisely evaluating the gifts of others is essential for every elder.

Body Life

A third element essential to the framework for elders to have is a thorough knowledge of Body Life. Elders and pastors set the example and provide the environment for Body Life in the local church. But what is Body Life?

When believers in the local church begin to discover and employ their spiritual gifts, serving one another and the community around them, something magnificent begins to happen: the local body of Christ literally comes alive, in a metamorphosis known as "Body Life."

Paul describes this transformation in Ephesians 4:1–16, especially in verses 11 through 16.

> **And He gave some as apostles, and some as prophets, and some as evangelists, and some as pastors and teachers, for the equipping of the saints for the work of service, to the building up of the body of Christ; until we all attain to the unity of the faith, and of the knowledge of the Son of God, to a mature man, to the measure of the stature which belongs to the fulness of Christ. As a result, we are no longer to be children,**

tossed here and there by waves, and carried about by every wind of doctrine, by the trickery of men, by craftiness in deceitful scheming; but speaking the truth in love, we are to grow up in all aspects into Him, who is the head, even Christ, from whom the whole body, being fitted and held together by that which every joint supplies, according to the proper working of each individual part, causes the growth of the body for the building up of itself in love.

In his well-known book on this subject, *Body Life,* Ray Stedman defined the phenomenon this way:

The church is primarily and fundamentally a body designed to express through each individual member the life of an indwelling Lord and is equipped by the Holy Spirit with gifts designed to express that life. (p. 5)

The emphasis is on "a body designed to express through each individual member the life of an indwelling Lord." The key to Body Life is for everyone to know his or her spiritual gifts, to be available to Christ that He might express His life through them, and to look to serve others rather than looking for one's own needs to be met.

When the Spirit of God begins to move in an entire church body in this way, to transform that body of people into a living organism that is the incarnate Body of Christ, the life unleashed is resurrection life no tomb can hold, not even the tomb of anti-Christian America in this amoral era. The final impact of such Body Life is the degree of maturity in every man and woman who enters into the fulness of humanity as God designed it to be—a stable, loving, truth-speaking stature, measuring up to the fulness of our risen Christ.

But when a church is bottlenecked by leadership that fails to understand that the ministry belongs to each individual member, what follows is body death, not body life. Stedman demonstrates how this happens:

> *It follows that there could hardly be anything more abortive or pathetic than a church which fails to understand this and substitutes instead the business methods, organizational proceedings, and pressure politics of the world to accomplish its work. That is a certain recipe for frustration and ultimate death.*

A church will soon die under the weight of unshared leadership and unfulfilled ministry unless the elders and pastoral leadership have a clear understanding of Body Life, and look to foster a ministry owned by each individual member. When elders begin to catch God's vision for how the Body of Christ is to function, and the Body comes alive, then the elders will watch God fulfill one of their highest callings—to bring that Body to maturity corporately by maturing believers individually. If you want to know where the joy of pastoral ministry is found . . . this is it!

Spiritual Warfare

But once the Body begins to come alive, the evil one notices and tries to squelch and destroy that life. He is a destroyer from the beginning, and we as elders must know his wily ways. If we fail to understand the fundamentals of spiritual warfare, we will be ambushed, and many of the sheep we serve will be hurt.

Elders must be wise warriors, understanding the dynamics of the battles we will face, that we may withstand the onslaught when the evil day arrives. This is a part of the framework of the elder's ministry most of us would like to overlook, but we discount it at our own peril.

To understand spiritual warfare, we must turn to Ephesians 6:10–18:

> **Finally, be strong in the Lord, and in the strength of His might. Put on the full armor of God, that you may be able to stand firm against the schemes of the devil. For our struggle is not against flesh and blood, but against the rulers, against the powers, against the world-forces of this darkness, against the spiritual forces of wickedness in the heavenly places. Therefore, take up the full armor of God, that you may be able to resist in the evil day, and having done everything, to stand firm. Stand firm therefore, having girded your loins with truth, and having put on the breastplate of righteousness, and having shod your feet with the preparation of the gospel of peace; in addition to all, taking up the shield of faith with which you will be able to extinguish all the flaming missiles of the evil one. And take the helmet of salvation, and the sword of the Spirit, which is the word of God. With prayer and petition pray at all times in the Spirit, and with this in view, be on the alert with all perseverance and petition for all the saints.**

The most striking theme of this passage is *stand firm.* Those two words appear three times, in verses 11, 13, and 14. The battle is unlike any other. This is a battle best joined as we close our eyes in prayer, standing firm in the truth of Scripture and in all the armor God supplies. We can wisely learn to thrust and parry with the Word of God, and by resting in our ultimate secret weapon— the victory which Christ has already attained, and in which we share.

This last point is often what tricks us. Because the war is already won by our great Captain, we tend to discount the ongoing battle. But it is very real, and this battle rages more for elders, pastors in the local church, and other leaders than it does for people in the congregation. This is because the enemy wants to destroy leaders and, by their downfall, discourage and dismantle the rest of the Body.

It is crucial for every elder to know that when the Holy Spirit makes him an overseer in his local church, he wears a large target on which the enemy's giant sights are leveled. Each elder will face the sniper fire of discouragement, often when he is tired and feeling alone at night. Each elder will have to endure the hail of bullets of criticism, when even his friends and family members will openly call his leadership into question. Each elder will face the buckshot of the multiple problems that all hit him on the same day or week, when shrapnel from church and home tear him apart simultaneously. Each elder will face the poison gas of deception, making him question what he knows to be true. And each elder will face the deprivations common to the battlefield—a lack of sleep at times, a lack of support from others in his unit, a lack of encouragement. Every elder reading this knows intimately the various aspects of this warfare, and every elder knows he must walk wisely through this battlefield.

As Corrie ten Boom said, "Don't wrestle, just nestle." Intimacy with God is what it boils down to, even for elders who are the veterans of many a campaign.

Family Life

Now we come to the final part of the framework of what an elder needs to know. He needs to be an accomplished family man. That is obvious from the two passages detailing the qualifications of an elder, 1 Timothy 3 and Titus 1. In this day of the disintegration of the family, it is especially important to summarize how an elder must first shepherd his family before he turns to shepherd the Body.

Here is an outline each elder may want to study and master for understanding the foundation of the Christian home:

- An elder is a loving husband.   Ephesians 5:18–33

- An elder is a father and a priest.   Ephesians 6:1–4

- An elder is a teacher and example.   Deuteronomy 6:4–9

- An elder is a wise parent,   Proverbs 2:1–22
  teaching wisdom.

- An elder is a wise mentor, who
  imparts:
    truth about sex;   Proverbs 5:1–23
    truth about relationships;   Proverbs 7:1–27
    truth about living life wisely.   Proverbs 1–9

Note that this outline begins with the elder having a clear understanding of God's call on his marriage. More specifically, the passage about marriage does not begin with the traditional starting point in verse 22 but with the logical linguistic antecedents in verses 18 through 21. In each case, this outline provides an extensive framework for understanding what an elder is called to be at home, so that he will not sacrifice his home life for his church office.

Having covered the five major parts of the framework an elder needs to know, the pragmatic question arises: What is the best way for elders not only to come to understand each of the five areas, but to *master* each one?

Learning What an Elder Needs to Know—Teach It!

Here's the best answer to that question: elders will learn this framework by *teaching* the relevant biblical passages to each other and evaluating one another.

Much good comes from this model. The first great benefit is that each teaching assignment forces the elder to study the passages seriously and diligently, because he knows he will be critiqued by his peers. The second great benefit is that all the elders will be in the teacher's chair at one point, and thus all will face similar tasks and challenges together, for the good of the whole. A wonderful *esprit de corps* develops as each man steps up, does his homework, gives the presentation, and then listens and responds to the critique. Before long, elders become men of the Word, bonded together in the common quest to know God's truth and to apply it well in His church.

Elders would do well to study the following passages, based on our previous discussion.

"Christ in you:"	Ezekiel 36:26–28
	Luke 22:20
	John 7:37–39
	John 14–16
	Romans 2:28–29
	Romans 8
	2 Corinthians 3:5–6
	Colossians 1:27
	Romans 1–8 (overview)
	2 Corinthians 2–4
Spiritual Gifts:	1 Peter 4:7–11
	1 Corinthians 12–14
	Romans 12:1–8
	Ephesians 4:1–16
Body Life:	Ephesians 4:1–16
Spiritual Warfare:	Ephesians 6:10–18

Family Life:
                                    Ephesians 5:18–33
                                    Ephesians 6:1–4
                                    Deuteronomy 6:4–9
                                    Proverbs 2:1–22
                                    Proverbs 5:1–23
                                    Proverbs 7:1–27
                                    Proverbs 1–9 (overview)

Here is a model set of instructions from one church that implemented this learning-by-teaching-each-other model.

Instructions for Expository Teaching

1. The task is to prepare a complete presentation of the passage in a 20-minute timeframe. This may mean a private rehearsal beforehand to stay within the allotted time.

2. Each elder will be critiqued by his peers (who hopefully will demonstrate grace) according to the following criteria:

- Did he cover the whole text?
- Did he clearly present the central truth of the text?
- Did he biblically support his conclusions?
- Did he apply his conclusions to practical life?
- Did he illustrate the truths he found from his own life?

Don't critique such things as style, stuttering, mannerisms, beads of sweat on the forehead, whiteness of face, or emotions (speaker or audience).

3. Each person should do his own work, even though the temptation to plagiarize from some great expositor will be great. Keep in mind that for your audience to be hooked on the passage, *you*

must be hooked on the passage. Don't neglect the powerful weapon of prayer!

As a final note of encouragement, we offer this prayer:

Our gracious Lord Jesus, may we elders study God's Word, the ultimate handbook on shepherding Your flock. May we read the passages on eldership over and over again, teaching them to one another and to the Body, until they are woven into our minds and hearts. May we then study and teach the passages about "Christ in you," spiritual gifts, Body Life, spiritual warfare, and family life to one another, building the necessary framework for every elder to master. And may we always remain available to You, our Chief Shepherd, to equip us from Your Word to know what elders need to know.

In Jesus' great Name, Amen!

PART II:

Elders: Practices and Procedures

CHAPTER SEVEN

The Importance of Listening

Since Jesus Christ is our Lead Man, the only one with all power and authority in heaven and on earth (Matthew 28:18), we are called to serve Him. That sounds so straightforward. But in practice, the art of servant leadership is as difficult to master as the art of parenting, or the art of loving one's wife. How do we begin to serve as servant leaders?

Let's ask the question in a more pointed way: how did Jesus Christ learn to be a servant leader? His remarkable new vision for leadership, revealed on that uphill journey to Jerusalem, did not arise out of nothing. His statement was over thirty years in the making. Jesus was the perfect model of a servant leader, both in washing the disciples' feet and in dying on the cross—the ultimate cleansing of sinners.

How did He come to understand this idea of servant leadership? How did He learn to lead as a servant? The answer to these questions does not lie in the Gospels, although certain insights may be gleaned from them. The answer can best be found in the prophetic visions of Isaiah, which are known as the Servant Songs. In the third Servant Song, found in Isaiah 50:4–11, we discover how God the Father taught Jesus the first step of servant leadership: *listening*.

Over the past fifteen years, I have had close contact with four different elder boards. Each board has had certain strengths and weaknesses. One elder board reflected a tradition of solid eldership which it had inherited from a generation of godly men. They appreciated the blessings and pitfalls of that inheritance. This board excelled in being circumspect about their past as they envisioned their future. A second elder board excelled in humility. A third excelled in spending time together as brothers, going the extra mile to create unity through brotherhood. The fourth elder board was the godliest group of men I have ever known, some of whom were elders for forty years. Sitting and watching these godly men, and being invited to take part in their meetings as a college student, was one of the richest spiritual experiences of my life. These men excelled in listening—listening to the Lord through prayer and listening to the Lord as each man shared what the Spirit was putting on his heart about each issue.

Indeed, listening to the Lord defines the godly and spiritual elder board. The converse is also true: not listening to the Lord defines the fleshly elder board. One board I knew was approached by two staff members, an entire deacon board, and one Sunday school teacher about their erratic and unbiblical leadership. The board circled the wagons and defended each other to the bitter end. Rather than humbly listening for the voice of the living Christ speaking through His people, they completely refused to listen.

Although more examples could be given to underscore this, most of us would agree that few elder boards have mastered the art of listening for the voice of the Lord of the church. Moreover, most of us would agree that we want to be part of an elder team that excels at listening to the Lord as He reveals His mind for His church.

Most elder boards struggle with this issue of listening. So do I. There is something that seems passive about listening. It flies in the face of our vision of the aggressive, take-the-hill type of leader. Most of us leave no time to listen to God, because pressing decisions demand our attention now. But if we forget to listen, to take time to pray and wait, to rest and give our Lord time to communicate His heart and mind to us, we will inevitably resort to fleshly leadership with all its political expediencies and power plays.

Let's see how Jesus Christ learned to listen.

The most mysterious period of Jesus' life is known as the "silent years." Those years are largely bypassed by all four Gospel writers. Luke does describe Jesus' intriguing session with the Temple teachers when he was twelve, and then Jesus reappears on the scene to be baptized by John when he was roughly thirty years old. What was happening during those eighteen years?

I have become convinced by both the third Servant Song of Isaiah and by various hints in the Gospels that Jesus was matriculated in God's School of Listening during those silent years. Long before Jesus learned to speak to great crowds, years before His sermons began with the compelling words "Blessed are the poor in spirit, for theirs is the kingdom of heaven," Jesus was learning how to listen.

Though the Gospels are silent about these years of quiet preparation, God allowed Isaiah to envision this school Jesus was in. Writing over six hundred years before Christ, Isaiah chronicled God's method of preparing the servant leader in the School of Listening. Here is how Isaiah describes that school in chapter 50:4–5:

The Lord GOD has given Me the tongue of disciples, that I may know how to sustain the weary one with a word. He awakens Me morning by morning, He awakens My ear to listen as a disciple. The Lord GOD has opened my ear; and I was not disobedient, nor did I turn back.

Again and again I have returned to this passage as one of the most important insights into how Jesus functioned. It reveals the secret behind the most arresting character quality of Christ—His uncanny ability to say exactly the right word at exactly the right time . . . every time. You cannot read any one of the Gospels for five minutes without being utterly amazed by Jesus' laser-like word power. From this Word came the word that pierces even between the hidden boundary of soul and spirit. How did He always know what to say, when it seems like most of us merely mumble and stutter our way through life?

Isaiah's simple answer is that God taught Jesus to listen for years before He gave Jesus even one public word to speak. We learn in John 8:28 and 12:50 that Jesus never spoke on His own initiative. His words were like arrows because His inner ear was tuned to His Father. And He had been trained in this process every day for years.

It is clear that from the time Jesus awoke each morning, the Father was in vital communication with Him. Jesus was His Father's disciple (Isaiah 50:4). The word *disciple* here could also be translated as "learner." He was a lifelong, day-in-and-day-out learner, and He learned by listening. The Father knew that if He had Jesus' ear in the morning, He had the whole man, and everything would follow after throughout the day.

Just what did Jesus hear in those early morning sessions in the School of Listening? He learned literally everything He needed to know for His three-year mission on earth!

We can discover how God laid out a roadmap for Christ's ministry by looking at the Servant Songs of Isaiah. For example, if Jesus wondered how He would achieve justice, the Father told Him it would be through compassion.

> **A bruised reed He will not break, and a dimly burning wick He will not extinguish; He will faithfully bring forth justice.**
>
> *Isaiah 42:3*

If Jesus wondered about the extent of the salvation God would bring through Him, and how He fit into God's covenant plans, the Father told Him the salvation would extend around the globe.

> **And now says the LORD, who formed Me from the womb to be His Servant, to bring Jacob back to Him, in order that Israel might be gathered to Him (for I am honored in the sight of the LORD, and My God is My strength), He says, "It is too small a thing that You should be My Servant to raise up the tribes of Jacob, and to restore the preserved ones of Israel; I will also make You a light of the nations so that My salvation may reach to the end of the earth."**
>
> *Isaiah 49:4–6*

The Father also revealed the staggering price to be paid for the salvation Jesus would win—the suffering at Calvary.

> **He was despised, and we did not esteem Him. Surely our griefs He Himself bore, and our sorrows He carried; yet we ourselves esteemed Him stricken, smitten of God, and afflicted. But He was pierced through for our transgressions, He was crushed for our iniquities; the chastening for our well-being fell upon Him, and by His scourging we are healed.**
>
> *Isaiah 53:3–5*

And foreseeing the joyful news of Jesus' victorious resurrection, the Father told Him He would inaugurate the reality of jubilee.

> **The Spirit of the Lord God is upon Me, because the Lord has anointed Me to bring good news to the afflicted; He has sent Me to bind up the brokenhearted, to proclaim liberty to captives, and freedom to prisoners; to proclaim the favorable year of the Lord.**

> *Isaiah 61:1–2*

The point of underscoring these passages is this: God fully disclosed to Jesus Christ everything He needed to know, and Jesus listened.

Right about now you may be saying to yourself, "Well sure, that is all fine and good for Jesus, the God-Man. But I am all too human, distracted by my daily life, beset by problems at home and at church—how on earth will all this work for me?"

In exactly the same way! Jesus set aside the independent exercise of His attributes as God to walk as man was meant to walk—by faith in the Father. Jesus was not operating out of His deity, rather He learned to be all that God intended for man to be by learning to listen, believe, and obey. Jesus learned everything He needed to know about His mission on earth not because He was divine, but because He listened.

God awakened Jesus' ear to listen, and then God filled Jesus' ear with all the direction He needed. This was not because Jesus was the "exceptional case." God also eagerly desires to awaken our ears, and to fill our ears with His direction. The God who went out of His way to communicate with Israel through dreams, visions, burning bushes, pillars of cloud, pillars of fire, prophets, Shekinah glories, the Urim and the Thummin, the casting of lots, the written Law and the Prophets, and, ultimately, the living Word, has proven Himself a ready and willing communicator.

The problem does not lie with God—it lies with us. We simply get too busy or feel too self-important to listen.

This theme is highly significant in the Scriptures. The entire book of Jeremiah is one exhaustive cautionary tale about the folly of not listening to God. And in the New Testament, God chose a highly strategic moment to communicate the importance of listening to Jesus Christ—just after the Transfiguration.

And a voice came out of the cloud, saying, "This is My Son, My Chosen One; listen to Him!" (Luke 9:35).

What other response is there to the Word? The Word must be heard and obeyed. All of this may seem quite elementary, like "Eldership 101." Nothing, however, is as quickly forgotten in the trench warfare of eldering in the local church. Complaints come in like floodwaters, ministry brushfires rage on all borders, and the pressure is on when all are looking to the elders to make some decision—*any* decision. That is just the moment when our top priority of listening falls like a lead weight to the bottom of the "Elder To Do" list. Suddenly we find ourselves reacting in the flesh rather than responding to the Spirit by prayer and listening.

Again, Jesus shows the way. In that remarkable story in Mark 1:32–39, Jesus shows us how to respond when the pressure is on.

> And when evening had come, after the sun had set, they began bringing to Him all who were ill and those who were demon-possessed. And the whole city had gathered at the door. And He healed many who were ill with various diseases, and cast out many demons; and He was not permitting the demons to speak, because they knew who He was. And in the early morning, while it was still dark, He arose and went out and departed to a lonely place, and was praying there. And Simon and his companions hunted for Him; and they found Him, and said to Him, "Everyone is looking for You." And He said to them, "Let us go somewhere else

to the towns nearby, in order that I may preach there also; for that is what I came out for." And He went into their synagogues throughout all Galilee, preaching and casting out the demons.

What was Jesus doing that early morning, after an entire city had crowded to His door the night before? He was alone with the Father, praying—and listening.

Recently, I was inspired by the true stories of two men for whom listening to God was the first priority of each day. The first such man was Hudson Taylor. I read a stirring account of what was at Taylor's core in the book entitled *How to Worship Jesus Christ,* by Joseph S. Carroll. Here is Carroll's take on Hudson Taylor's spiritual secret:

> *What was it that made Hudson Taylor the man he became and was, right to the end? His son and daughter-in-law, who traveled constantly with him in his later years, testify that often they would be traveling over a hard cobblestone road for many hours in a springless cart. Arriving at a Chinese inn late at night, they would endeavor to obtain a little corner in a room for their father, Hudson Taylor; for usually in those inns there was just one large room where everybody slept. He was now an aged man; but, without fail, every morning just before dawn there would be the scratching of a match and the lighting of a candle, and Hudson Taylor would worship God. This was the key to his life. It was said that even before the sun rose on China, Hudson Taylor was worshiping God.*

Beyond a doubt, a key element of his worship was placing before God the offering of an open ear.

A. W. Tozer was also a listening man. Carroll recounts Tozer's life of listening:

When an acquaintance of mine, who was called to minister in Chicago, arrived in that city, A. W. Tozer called him and said, 'This city is a devil's den. It is a very difficult place to minister the Word of God, and you will come up against much opposition from the enemy. If you ever want to pray with me, I'm at the lakeside every morning at five-thirty. Just make your way down and we can pray together.' Not wanting to bother the great man as he was seeking the Lord, my acquaintance did not immediately accept his offer. But one day he was so troubled that he made his way very early to the lakeside, about six o'clock, only to find God's servant prostrate upon the sand worshiping God. Needless to say he did not disturb him.

Every elder wants to be a listening man as Jesus was—and as these great men of faith were. But how do we get there? Practically speaking, how do we actually listen to our Lord as elders?

First and foremost, we must be sure that we are "walking in the Spirit" (Galatians 5:16), "filled with the Spirit" (Ephesians 5:18), and immersing ourselves in the Word of God. Colossians 3:16 says, "Let the word of Christ dwell in you richly as you teach and admonish one another with all wisdom." When God speaks to us about anything, it will always be in complete agreement with His written Word and by the power of the Holy Spirit.

But what about real-life situations? Although the Spirit will lead different men to listen to Him in unique ways, here are some examples.

One man would get up early, before the day started, and take the current elder meeting agenda and lay it on the table before the Lord. Taking the first item on the agenda, he would read the item to the Lord, and then ask Him, "Lord, what do You think about this? What do You want?" And he sat quietly before the Lord, listening through the Spirit and the Word. He would then write down some of the thoughts and reasoning that would infuse his mind during those minutes of listening. After a few minutes on agenda item number one, he would move on and read the second item to the Lord, and listen for a while about that item. Each day between elder meetings he would do this—it was his "homework." After a week or so, sitting and patiently listening, he usually came to a clear sense of what the Lord was telling him about each item on the agenda. By listening to his Lord, his quest to find the mind of Christ was well-rewarded.

Another brother would take the roster of all those who attended the church, and he would lay it before the Lord, praying through each member by name, from the newest newborn to the oldest senior citizen. As this brother prayed, he would ask the Lord specific questions about each member so that he could better minister to them. He would then allow for an interval of silence—listening. This brother was seeking the mind of Christ, not just in a general sense, but in a specific and personal sense—the mind of Christ for that particular person by name. This is another realm of listening.

Similarly, one elder who was also a pastor in his church would come in early every Sunday morning and take the church roster and pray through each name before standing up to teach them. By simply saying each name before the Lord, and then listening to what the Lord might say, or by considering the thoughts or impressions put on his heart, he was equipped to see them and talk to them later that morning. More importantly he was prepared to stand before them to deliver their weekly meal from the Word of God.

Some elders might take the meeting agenda, lay it beside the open Word of God, and see how the Lord might be speaking to them from the pages of Scripture. For these men, listening to the Spirit may well come in the form of listening to the Word.

Other elders might take prayer walks, to talk with the Lord and to listen as He speaks to their hearts when they are outside, beyond the normal confines of their daily lives. For some men, it is easier to hear from the Lord out in nature. This was certainly true of Jesus—who knows how many nights He spent up on the mountain, in the cold dark quiet—listening.

Who knows how He will guide each one of us to listen to Him in a unique way, tailored to our personality? He is a ready communicator. May our great God teach us every morning in the School of Listening, and may our living Christ enable us to listen and obey our Father.

CHAPTER EIGHT

Unanimity and the Mind of Christ

Let's return to Peninsula Bible Church. In the fall of 1971, I was still under assignment as a management consultant to help them in specific areas. It was a time when the Jesus movement was in full swing and PBC was growing by leaps and bounds. Something was happening at the church from dawn until dusk, and many times late into the evening as well.

This increased activity began to affect the neighbors adversely. People who wanted to spend a quiet afternoon in their yards were disturbed by car doors slamming, loud voices, and exhaust wafting over the fence from the previously-quiet church facility. On the side streets surrounding the church, people would park their cars so that bumpers overlapped driveways. Thus, during two—and sometimes three—services, local residents couldn't even leave their own homes.

Finally the neighborhood got together and 144 families signed a petition addressed to the city council which said, in effect, that Peninsula Bible Church was a nuisance to the community.

When the elders got a copy of the petition, along with notice of a formal hearing on the matter, full attention was devoted to the problem.

As the process went on, the elders appointed me as their representative to the city council. *That* was an interesting assignment! The first time I went to the city council, there was considerable hostility directed toward the church. In fact, the mayor explained that, in his judgment, our particular church caused such irritation in the community that the good done by the church barely balanced out the bad. He went on to say that if we got any larger or added any more activities, the city might cancel the permit that let the church occupy property in a residential (R1) zone.

I tried to point out the good PBC was doing in the community. Although the council graciously listened to specific examples supporting my premise, their attitude didn't soften. At the end of the meeting, one councilman made a proposal that PBC should limit growth as controlled by the number of services and the number of seats in the auditorium. He further suggested that a decision was necessary within two weeks so that the city council could pacify the neighbor's complaints.

At the next board of elders meeting, I explained this dire situation. For two hours I watched the elders go back and forth in their discussion. From time to time I would remind them of the seriousness of this decision and urge them to get on with it. In the end, there was still no clear consensus as to what to do. We couldn't even formulate a majority opinion! Finally the moderator requested a special meeting to discuss the matter further. He urged everyone to pray and to ask the Lord for guidance.

A few days later the special meeting took place. Once again I watched the same process. This time all the elders seemed to be in agreement to challenge the city's demand and not give in to the world's pressure on the church of Jesus Christ. But the elders were very concerned about the situation with the neighbors.

A number of elders urged a visit to every neighbor to apologize personally for any inconvenience caused by the church. Furthermore, we discussed the need to instruct the congregation not to infringe on neighbor's driveways and to be especially considerate of them. It appeared that there was a clear majority of elders who felt this was the right approach to take.

But when the moderator took the vote, one elder disagreed.

Several elders began questioning the man to see what he was basing his position upon. His reply was simply, "Gentlemen, I just don't feel right about this decision." I could tell that some of the other guys were a bit frustrated, but he wouldn't budge. Finally the moderator said, "Gentlemen, I'm sorry we can't reach a decision tonight because we have chosen only to decide things on the basis of unanimous agreement, and one elder here isn't ready to decide."

Immediately I stood and said, "Gentlemen, you don't realize the seriousness of this matter. You must make a decision tonight because the governmental power in charge has insisted that you make a decision and the two weeks are almost up."

I didn't say it out loud, but privately I thought that this dear brother was just being obstinate. He certainly didn't present his case as well as Ray Stedman, or Bob Smith, or some of the other leading elders. Therefore, as any businessman should know, he ought to give way to the more dynamic men and not hold up the decision-making process.

I felt this was doubly true since this crucial decision had to be made so the city council would appreciate our serious response to their request. Instead, the moderator turned to me and said, "I'm sorry, we simply can't reach a decision. You're going to have to tell the city council we can't respond to their request in the time limit they have given us."

I left the meeting thinking, "The elders are really in for it! If we get on the negative side of the city council we have no hope of negotiating with them for some middle ground. They'll step in and begin to control the activities of Peninsula Bible Church."

It seemed to me that these elders had an archaic way of making decisions. Didn't they know that you can't run an organization with such a ponderous method as "unanimity"? Modern organizations *must* have quick-decision making processes if they're going to function efficiently—or so I thought.

I attended the next city council meeting (though I considered leaving town). To my surprise, as soon as the mayor recognized me, he deviated from the proceedings to say, "I'm sorry Mr. Winslow, we will not be able to take up Peninsula Bible Church's situation this evening due to circumstantial changes, but please be prepared to come to the next meeting two weeks from now. Please accept my apologies for the inconvenience."

I couldn't believe it. Somehow the crisis I'd anticipated never occurred and there was still time for the elders to reach a decision. When I explained the situation to the elders at their next regularly scheduled meeting, no one seemed surprised. I was astonished to find that in the two-week interval, something had changed the minds of all the elders so that there was a complete turnaround. Now everyone was in accord with the lone holdout from the last meeting. I was amazed. In a manner of minutes, everyone agreed that they should decide to let the city council limit the number of services and the number of seats in the auditorium. I began to question some of the guys, wondering if arms had been twisted somehow.

Each of my queries was answered basically the same way.

"We felt that the Spirit of God wanted us to decide this way."

"Well, did anybody put pressure on you? Did Stedman change his mind and urge all of the rest of you to follow his lead?"

"No, I simply prayed and this is what I feel God wants me to do."

I had never seen anything like this before. I wanted to find out what Scriptural principle these guys are using for this method of decision-making. So, with some help from Ray Stedman and Bob Smith, I turned to the Scriptures.

> **Therefore, I exhort the elders among you, as your fellow-elder and witness of the sufferings of Christ, and a partaker also of the glory that is to be revealed, shepherd the flock of God among you, not under compulsion, but voluntarily, according to the will of God; and not for sordid gain, but with eagerness; nor yet as lording it over those allotted to your charge, but proving to be examples to the flock.**
>
> *1 Peter 5:1–3*

Notice that elders are to "shepherd the flock of God among you [a local church], according to the will of God." This means the elders have the responsibility of finding the will of the head of the church. Jesus said, "I will build *my* church and the gates of hell will not prevail against it" (Matthew 16:18, italics added). He is the head of the church (Ephesians 1:22–23; Colossians 1:18).

Therefore, if elders are to shepherd according to the will of God, they must find out what the Head wants done for His church. So how do we find out what an unseen Head wants done in a particular church situation.

A helpful starting point is Acts 15:28. The setting was a momentous situation facing the early church—what to do with the gentile Christians. So they convened the council at Jerusalem, made up of elders and apostles, to seek the mind of the Lord.

Verse 28 says, "For it seemed good to the Holy Spirit and to us also." From the context we know that there was much discussion. They sought various opinions. They considered the Scripture.

They prayed. Finally, they reached a unanimous decision. "It seems good to us, having become of one mind" (v. 25). The final decision was made after all the discussion and after the witness of the Holy Spirit in each man's heart. This is what gave them the belief that they had the mind of the Lord. So they confidently declared it to be so for the whole church.

From a practical point of view, any time a group comes together to discuss a matter, initially there will be various points of view depending on background, temperament, knowledge, experience, and other variables. Under natural conditions unanimous agreement will not occur, and even a majority agreement will be difficult. To insist on true unanimity for a decision is to say, "We expect the Spirit of God to reach into the minds of one or more of the participants and change those minds or we will never reach a unanimous decision. Therefore, when we do reach a unanimous decision, we believe the Spirit of God has acted and thus we have the mind of the Lord for His church on this specific issue."

That is quite a concept. You surely wouldn't want to run a business that way. But it's a good way to run the church of Jesus Christ.

Standards for achieving unanimity

We suggest the following standards for elders in a local church to adopt in making unanimous decisions.

1. The participants in this unanimous decision-making process must be elders as defined in Acts 20:28.

In this verse the apostle Paul tells the elders at Ephesus that the Holy Spirit made them overseers of the church at Ephesus. In other words, elders aren't elders because of a popularity contest among the congregation or because they happen to have certain business experience. The Spirit of God must give them spiritual gifts for overseeing and shepherding and must assign them to the local church in which He has determined those spiritual gifts should be employed. Thus every elder must meet the spiritual and biblical qualifications given in 1 Timothy 3:1–7 and Titus 1:5–9. (See Chapter 2, p. 31 for more on these qualifications.)

2. All elders must be allowed to address the question at hand with complete freedom as brothers.

No arm-twisting allowed. No putting pressure on anyone. A senior pastor is not allowed to exert undue pressure on someone less theologically inclined than he is.

3. Each elder must speak to the issue based on what he believes in his heart that God is directing him to say.

It is not acceptable for an elder to say, "You guys go ahead and vote on this issue, I'll just pass." All must be charged with equal responsibility to seek the mind of the Lord individually. Thus, each person, with their unique background, experience, and knowledge contributes to the issue.

4. It only takes one person to stop any decision-making process.

There can be no attempt to coerce or manipulate others to come around to a particular point of view. If a decision cannot be reached with genuine unanimity, then the board remains immovable with no decision made until the Lord brings all the men to a unanimous decision.

Several conclusions may be drawn from these procedures.

• Every elder is required to seek the mind of the Lord personally for each particular situation. All elders must be involved in every decision so that later on no wedge can be driven between the elders who think differently on an issue. This removes a tool of Satan for disrupting and dividing local churches.

- A second result is that every elder knows in his heart God has acted because the decision making process required faith that God's Spirit would bring about the unanimous decision. As a result, the elders move about the local church demonstrating a confidence and faith that the Lord Himself is directing this church. Moreover, this confidence and faith does wonders for the saints in that local assembly, instilling confidence and assurance in their hearts.

- This procedure makes evident the wisdom of God when the wisdom of man simply cannot suffice.

Sometime after I became an elder in a local church, a pastor to minister in the area of music and worship was needed. One of the leaders immediately suggested a talented young man ministering in a town nearby. All of the elders took time to go and observe his ministry and get to know him personally. Over a period of two or three months, almost everyone became convinced he was God's man for us. In fact, many were very sure that we should act promptly or another church would snatch him out from underneath our noses. Finally, when the vote came, all were positive for extending him an offer except one lone elder.

Over the next several months the subject was brought up at each elder meeting, and still there was no unanimous decision. After a while it became obvious that we couldn't act until God got around to finally changing this man's mind. In the meantime, we continued to suffer in the church from not having a music pastor. Finally we started looking at other candidates, but without success.

Interestingly, at the same time several elders who were close to the first candidate began to report that things were not going well in his life. At the very time we were looking at him, his wife had fallen into adultery and he himself had acted inappropriately within his own marriage. Eventually they got a divorce and he went through a real time of discipline from the Lord.

As the years passed, the Lord brought him to the end of himself and taught him real humility. As he began to recover, he went back to school for further biblical training and, as he himself tells it, he learned to depend on the Lord rather than his flashy talents.

Four and one-half years later one of the elders reintroduced this young man's name for our consideration and filled us in on all that had taken place since. Once more all of the elders contacted this candidate again and renewed their relationship with him. When the vote was called, we had unanimous agreement immediately and that gentleman and the new family that God gave him have been ministering in that church for the last fifteen years to God's glory.

As I think back on this example, truly the Spirit of God knew things that we could never have known as human beings. Through this procedure of unanimous agreement He built his church the way He wanted to do it.

CHAPTER NINE

The Discipleship of Shepherds

Sometime after joining the staff of Peninsula Bible Church, I was contacted by several men from a medium-sized church that was experiencing a high staff turnover rate. These men asked if I could visit with them for a couple of days and perhaps give them some advice.

When I arrived in their city, I was immediately taken to a large meeting room in a local bank. There I met eighteen elders plus the senior pastor and three associate pastors. Everyone was seated in a large circle. After the introductions, the whole group looked at me as if to say, "Well . . . ?" Since the ball was clearly in my court I started out by saying, "Gentlemen, I'd like to talk to you as a consultant, not as a church expert of any kind. Consultants, as I define the term, only have two things to offer, objectivity and time—brains are not all that important. A consultant spends time asking questions to pull out what is really going on. Then he tries to get everyone thinking objectively about the issues—although he may synthesize things somewhat—so that finally, all arrive at wise solutions to the problems that exist. Therefore, please do not be offended by my questions. My first question is: What are the three greatest problems in your church?"

One of the older men said, "Well, we've been growing, so our facilities are too small. We need to build bigger facilities to accommodate this growth, and we want to grow even faster."

"That certainly covers at least three problems. Why do you think you need to grow?"

"Well, because everybody knows you have to grow."

"Has the Lord told you that you have to grow?"

"Well, no, but everyone knows that if an organization doesn't grow, it stagnates and dies."

"That's the way secular organizations are, but can you show me in Scripture where the church will die if it doesn't grow numerically?"

For a moment, there was silence as everyone looked at the senior pastor to see what he would say. Then the atmosphere turned to laughter as the men identified with the fellow on the hot-seat trying to think through the difference between churches and secular organizations.

"Maybe what I ought to ask is, What has God called your church to do as an organization? Do you have evangelistic services, altar calls? Do you send members out into the community to bring the lost in to your facilities to be saved?"

Several men said, "No, we don't do any of those things."

"Then what do you do?"

The senior pastor said, "We basically teach the Scripture to believers. Now some of our people are involved in an evangelism program for their neighbors."

"Do they bring their neighbors to your church?"

"No, all the work of the program goes on in people's homes."

"Then it seems to me that God has not called you as an organization to be an evangelistic arm of His Body. Is that right?"

After considerable discussion, most agreed that was the case.

"Well, if that's true, could it be possible that what God wants you to be is just a section of pipe. Baby Christians come in one end of the pipe, you help them to mature by teaching them the Scriptures and help them discover their spiritual gifts, then God takes them out the other end of the pipe and sends them where He wants them to minister. In the meantime, you stay the same size numerically, and you find that all the time and effort you would spend searching for land, building new buildings (arguing about how to tear down your barns and build larger), is not His plan at all."

One man immediately said, "Hey, you know that's right! I was working with Joe and Ann and now they've gone to another ministry on the other side of town. Also, you remember that other couple who was here for a while and now have moved to another state. This does seem to be what God is doing."

Quite a discussion ensued, with the senior pastor frequently correcting statements and commenting on the idea of the Lord being the boss of His church. Interestingly, none of the associate pastors said anything.

At that point, I changed the subject. "How are decisions made in your church?"

The senior pastor explained that they made decisions on a unanimous basis after much prayer. They felt the Lord was directing them through this procedure.

I turned to them and asked, "Do each of you take time to think through the problems that need solutions?"

Once more the senior pastor started to answer. I interrupted him and said, "Excuse me, but since you've asked me to lead this evaluation, I'd like to make an observation. You have been answering most of the questions I've been asking. I'd like to make a proposal. For the next five or six minutes you simply keep quiet. I don't want to offend you, but I'd like to address your men to see what they think."

He looked startled but being a good sport said, "OK."

"Also, we need to ask you to turn your chair away from the group so they won't see your expressions, OK?"

He graciously agreed. During the next five minutes, as I asked questions about how they made decisions, guys would lean over to see what the senior pastor's facial expression was before they would answer. It became evident that what these elders were used to doing was, in someone's words, "lie in the weeds" until they saw which way the senior pastor was going to jump; then everybody voted that way. One man came right out and said who the boss was: it was the senior pastor.

He said, "We depend on him; everybody's got to report to him."

At this point I said to the men, "It seems to me that God has really called you to help believers mature and now you men are beginning to say that you're convinced that's what He wants you to do. So, if you're the leaders of this church, it would seem like you ought to be the ones who are shepherding and discipling believers."

Everyone said, "We don't know how."

"Well, what do you have the senior pastor doing?"

It turned out that the senior pastor did all the counseling, all the visiting of the sick, made most of the decisions, had all staff members reporting to him. He even turned out the lights at night.

"Let me suggest something. Suppose you cancel all the senior pastor's assignments except two. First, we ask him to preach on Sundays. Second, we ask him to disciple all of you elders. What do you think about that?"

All of a sudden men were getting excited about that possibility. Finally, everybody agreed (except the mum senior pastor), that the finest thing that could happen would be to have the senior pastor equip them all for ministry.

"The real question now is, Will you men commit to being disciples, that is, to give the time and energy necessary so discipleship has a high priority in your life?"

They all said yes!

"Now let's ask our senior pastor."

His answer was wonderful: "If you men really want me to disciple you, it would change my whole life. I'd really do it, I really would!"

This fits exactly with the apostle Paul's word to churches in Ephesians 4:11–16:

> And He gave some as apostles, and some as prophets, and some as evangelists, and some as pastors and teachers, for the equipping of the saints for the work of service, to the building up of the body of Christ; until we all attain to the unity of the faith, and of the knowledge of the Son of God, to a mature man, to the measure of the stature which belongs to the fullness of Christ.
>
> As a result, we are no longer to be children, tossed here and there by waves, and carried about by every wind of doctrine, by the trickery of men, by craftiness in deceitful scheming; but speaking the truth in love, we are to grow up in all aspects into Him, who is the head, even Christ, from whom the whole body, being fitted and held together by that which every joint supplies, according to the proper working of each individual part, causes the growth of the body for the building up of itself in love.

Notice that the leaders of the church, regardless of how they are gifted, have a purpose and a goal that leads to a result. The purpose is to equip the saints—that's the ordinary believers—for serving and building up the Body (v. 12).

The goal is that we all are unified in our faith, mature in our knowledge of the Son of God, and have reached the capacity of appropriating all of Christ in everything we do (v. 13).

The result is that we are no longer immature and subject to all kinds of false doctrines, but are speaking the truth in love (vv. 14–16). We grow spiritually, depending entirely on Christ, our head. This makes it possible for the whole body of Christians to work together in harmony, each one serving the other in love and utilizing their spiritual gifts to build up others in the Body.

The foregoing paraphrase of this text implies that pastors, especially older pastors, have the special privilege of equipping elders to minister among the saints in a local church. They should view this assignment with high priority and excuse themselves from all the busy work which so easily distracts.

Paul shows how to disciple elders in Acts 20:17–38:

> **And from Miletus he sent to Ephesus and called to him the elders of the church. And when they had come to him, he said to them, "You yourselves know, from the first day that I set foot in Asia, how I was with you the whole time, serving the Lord with all humility and with tears and with trials which came upon me through the plots of the Jews; how I did not shrink from declaring to you anything that was profitable, and teaching you publicly and from house to house, solemnly testifying to both Jews and Greeks of repentance toward God and faith in our Lord Jesus Christ.**

> **And now, behold, bound in spirit, I am on my way to Jerusalem, not knowing what will happen to me there,**

except that the Holy Spirit solemnly testifies to me in every city, saying that bonds and afflictions await me. But I do not consider my life of any account as dear to myself, in order that I may finish my course, and the ministry, which I received from the Lord Jesus, to testify solemnly of the gospel of the grace of God.

And now, behold, I know that you all, among whom I went about preaching the kingdom, will see my face no more. Therefore I testify to you this day, that I am innocent of the blood of all men. For I did not shrink from declaring to you the whole purpose of God. Be on guard for yourselves, and for all the flock, among which the Holy Spirit has made you overseers, to shepherd the church of God which He purchased with His own blood. I know that after my departure savage wolves will come in among you, not sparing the flock; and from among your own selves men will arise, speaking perverse things, to draw away the disciples after them. Therefore be on the alert, remembering that night and day for a period of three years I did not cease to admonish each one with tears.

And now I commend you to God and to the word of His grace, which is able to build you up and to give you the inheritance among all those who are sanctified. I have coveted no one's silver or gold or clothes. You yourselves know that these hands ministered to my own needs and to the men who were with me. In everything I showed you that my working hard in this manner you must help the weak and remember the words of the Lord Jesus, that He Himself said, "It is more blessed to give than to receive."

And when he had said these things, he knelt down and prayed with them all. And they began to weep aloud and embraced Paul, and repeatedly kissed him, grieving especially over the word, which he had spoken, that they should see his face no more. And they were accompanying him to the ship.

Acts 20:17–38

We may draw six principles for discipling elders from this passage.

1. Commitment to Individuals

Paul was with the leaders the whole time (v. 18). He was committed to them. In verse 31 he said that for three years he did not cease to admonish each one with tears. He really cared about these men who became elders of the church at Ephesus. They must have felt perfectly free to call on the apostle anytime they needed him.

2. Formal Teaching of Truth

In verse 20 the apostle explains that he taught them publicly. When was that? In Acts 19:9–10 we learn that he taught them daily for two years in the school of Tyrannus. He taught them "anything that was profitable," which was "the whole purpose of God" (v. 27).

What a thrill to have been taught by the apostle Paul! Scholars suggest they spent six hours a day, six days a week in study, poring over the Old Testament.

Do you suppose elders today need to be taught such overlooked passages as the ten great homilies of wise living from Proverbs? What would our churches be like if the elders and pastors would meet together each week to study God's Word? The apostle may have had the following goal in mind for teaching the elders of Ephesus.

And we proclaim Him, admonishing every man and teaching every man with all wisdom, that we may present every man complete in Christ. And for this purpose also I labor, striving according to His power, which mightily works within me.

Colossians 1:28–29

3. Demonstration by Example

In Colossians 1:20–21, the apostle took them with him as he went from house to house testifying to both Jews and Greeks about the gospel and preaching the kingdom (v. 25). In verse 35 he points out how he "showed them" how to serve and minister.

Jesus also demonstrated this principle with His disciples. He was constantly challenging them, testing them, and including them in His ministry.

Today a pastor should include his elders in his ministry. If he is asked to speak at a conference, he should take an elder along. Elders should be invited to participate with the pastor as he ministers to the sick, counsels couples for marriage, and conducts memorial services. It is good for an elder to preach on occasion.

4. Share Your Life

In verses 22–26 the apostle shares his thoughts and fears. He is open and vulnerable. Even though he was an apostle, he treated the elders as brothers, on the same level with him.

Jesus had to help His disciples see this truth when they were discussing which one of them was the greatest in Mark 9:33–37. He used a child to demonstrate humility and equality.

It is often difficult for pastors to be open with their elders. But if the first and second elements have been in place for some time, it can happen. If the pastor chooses to serve his elders (to make it a priority to minister to them), then the Holy Spirit will enhance their openness with each other.

5. Exhortation To Be On Guard

The apostle exhorts the leaders to be on guard in two ways:

For yourselves — First, an elder is responsible to the Holy Spirit. To no one else do you have a higher commitment because He made you overseers of the flock (v. 28).

Second, an elder must constantly communicate with the Lord (v. 32) because power to minister comes only from Him.

Finally, an elder must apply God's Word to himself (v. 32) before ever presenting it to the flock.

For all the flock — Impostors will try to carry the flock away with spurious doctrine and false ideas. False Christians will say perverse things to cause factions and trouble in the Body.

The implication from these two warnings is that the elders can expect the Holy Spirit to direct them as to what they should do in a particular situation. The flock isn't theirs, it belongs to the Lord Jesus, since He purchased it with His own blood.

6. Turn Them Loose

The apostle sends them forth (v. 32) to be built up, to receive the inheritance, and to be sanctified apart from his presence. He believes he will never see them again (v. 25), but he is convinced that God's grace will take care of them. He encourages them to follow his example.

- Remember to admonish people with love (v. 31).
- Use God's word, not man's ideas or procedures (v. 32).
- Judge your covetousness for what others have (v. 32).
- Work hard and give to others (vv. 34–35).

One of the hardest things to do is turn loose the men you have come to know and love. Yet God often assigns them elsewhere and they need to fly on their own. What a wonderful privilege it is for a pastor to disciple the elders God has given to the church he serves.

CHAPTER TEN

Stewardship of the Lord's Finances

A friend of mine who grew up in the Brethren tradition in the Pacific Northwest once said, "You can tell a godly man by how he handles money." The same can be said of an elder board: you can tell a godly elder board by how they manage the church finances.

The following story should caution us all. After serving as a pastor at a church for just over a year, the church secretary and I got into a conversation about finances. She knew the elders and I had been talking about the trend in weekly giving, which from January to June was running about 67 percent of the weekly need. I told the elders I was willing to "make tents" for a while in the business world until we got over this financial hiccup.

I had also asked the elders to consider other things we might do to improve the financial picture of the church. A trend of poor giving is often a tell-tale symptom of another problem in the church leadership—often some form of immorality at the top. We needed to look at this problem together.

My secretary was curious about the discussions regarding finances. I told her I would likely go back into the marketplace for a season, since the elders said there was no other solution.

She immediately protested: "That's just not true. There is at least $45,000 in three secret accounts within the church accounting structure."

She told me that three men who were not elders were giving large sums to be kept in an account designated for each man. They claimed the tax write-off, then called the secretary during the next twelve months with instructions to write checks to the ministries or individuals they designated. She wrote the checks, and one of the elders signed them. But some of those checks went to pay for things like hospital bills of their own families.

These men were using the church as a tax shelter. Although the secretary had spoken to the elder who signed the checks, he had done nothing.

I told my secretary I would immediately look into the problem and call a special elder meeting on Sunday afternoon. I called three experts from around the country and described our dilemma to them. One was a CPA who handled my own taxes and who advised at least one church on tax issues. Another individual was an experienced elder who had served his large church as the treasurer for almost twenty years. The third man was an elder and consultant who had set up church accounting systems for two different churches and who often advised elders and pastors on finance-related issues.

All three men agreed the practice was outside the tax code, and the church was in serious danger of losing its 501-(C)3 nonprofit status. One said, "This practice is not only illegal, you must confront the elders as soon as possible! If they do not immediately repent and redress this issue, you cannot stay at that church."

On the following Sunday, I called a special meeting and confronted the men about the problem. I recounted the secretary's concern and what my research had revealed. "This practice is illegal," I told them.

We had been studying eldership issues in the Bible, from Genesis to Revelation, for a year, every Tuesday morning from 6:00–8:00 a.m. One of our conclusions was that elders must serve the Lord with a pure heart. "As the leaders go, so goes the church." I felt the Lord was putting before us a test of all we had learned, and the elders' response to the statement "This practice is illegal" would reveal much about their hearts.

My statement hung in the air for a long time, until the elder who signed the checks finally spoke. "Well, I guess it's technically illegal," he said, "but I really don't have a problem with it."

I carefully explained the whole matter again. He responded, "Well, it's really more shady than it is illegal, but I'm sure a lot of other churches do it, and they probably do it worse than we do." The meeting went downhill from there. Nothing was accomplished and we all went outside afterward to light fireworks for our churchwide Fourth of July family picnic.

Three weeks later, while I was on vacation, the elders conducted a business meeting with the church body. At that meeting, they handed out an updated financial report.

When I got back from vacation, my secretary gave me two financial reports, both created on computer spreadsheets. One was the most recent financial report from before my vacation. The other one had been handed out while I was gone.

The report that was handed out while I was on vacation had been changed! Two line items had been completely deleted, even though the monies still remained in the secret accounts. The deleted items were "designated receipts" and "designated disbursements."

So after being confronted about an illegal financial practice, the elders' response was to doctor the financial reports distributed to the Body of Christ. Three days later, I resigned. The secretary resigned shortly thereafter. Less than a year later, the church closed its doors.

What a heartbreak! How did an elder who genuinely wanted to serve Jesus Christ allow an illegal financial practice to go on for years. Not only that, he then rationalized the practice when it was formally confronted, and ultimately took the far more serious step of lying to the Body of Christ?

How can we faithfully serve our Lord and the Body that is His church in this troubling area of finances? Here are some financial policies that have been implemented in several churches we have both served.

Paying Bills

1. The basic principle that is correct biblically and ethically is based on two procedures:

    a. We will take from zero to 30 days from the time of receipt of invoice, bill, or charge to pay all expenses incurred. If a bill goes beyond 30 days from receipt, that bill is overdue.

    b. If we ever have insufficient funds to meet overdue bills and salaries, then our procedure is to first pay the overdue bills, second pay the support staff (secretaries, maintenance personnel), and then, if the Lord does not miraculously provide the funds, the pastoral staff will take the necessary cut in their salaries to accommodate the shortage. The support staff will also take a paycut, but only as a last resort.

2. What constitutes an overdue bill?

   a. In today's business world, 30 days is the limit that companies allow customers to pay their bills. Most invoices threaten to charge interest and/or make collections for nonpayment past 30 days. Many suppliers even call when a bill has gone beyond 10 days.

      Everyone in the business world accepts that it takes time for the client company to process a bill and pay it. After a reasonable time has elapsed, the client has begun to conduct business with someone else's money.

   b. We as believers should not have late bills for two reasons.

      In Proverbs 3:27–28 wisdom says:

      Do not withhold good from those to whom it is due when it is in your power to do it. Do not say to your neighbor, "Go, and come again, and tomorrow I will give it"—when you have it with you.

   c. We should not withhold paying bills if we have money in the bank that we are holding for something else. What we are saying to our non-Christian neighbors (suppliers) is that we cannot trust the Lord to supply our needs.

      If we do not pay bills that have become overdue, and instead use that money for other purposes (such as payroll), we are operating the church on the world's money.

3. Suppose we use the money we have in the bank to pay the bills before they become overdue? Then we come to payroll with insufficient funds to cover the total payroll. What happens then? (Note: This has never happened in the history of our church.)

   a. Because the pastoral staff understands that their salaries are dependent on week-to-week giving from God's people, and have taught that we are all totally dependent on the Lord, they should be the first to accept the necessary cut in their monthly income.

b. It makes no difference how great the needs of the pastoral staff might be. Our whole premise is that the Lord will supply our needs, if not through the giving of His people, then through another means. If the pastoral staff has to be guaranteed their salary and the bills are not paid when money is on hand to do so, then something is decidedly wrong with the teaching.

c. If the Lord has brought us to the point where pastors' salaries must be cut, and yet it is necessary to cut even further, we may assume the Lord is saying to us that the organization must be revamped. Remember, it is still be better to impose a cut in salary for the entire staff than to operate with other people's money and disobey the clear statement of Proverbs 3.

Instructions for Signing Checks

By following these instructions, we should avoid confusion concerning the issue of checks, the proper signing of checks, and the speedy processing of all bills.

In many churches, the bookkeeper is the only signee. This means that he or she has the ultimate responsibility for paying all bills. As elders, we should carry that responsibility as the spiritual leaders and shepherds of the Body. Only the elders are aware of all that is going on in the church. Therefore, all checks should have two signatures—that of the bookkeeper and that of an elder.

Here is the procedure:

1. The bookkeeper should make out the check and sign it first. This indicates that the bookkeeper has properly prepared the check and that there are sufficient funds in the bank. The bookkeeper is responsible for knowing the account balances.

2. When the check is presented for an elder's signature, an invoice or other note must be attached which states the purpose of the check. The elder can then decide the validity of the expense.

3. All invoices or notes attached to checks must contain the initials of a responsible person who has approved the expense. This tells the elder whom he should go to with questions. The bookkeeper is never responsible for approving expenses.

The only exception to the above procedure concerns payroll checks. Payroll is established by the action of the elder board. The minutes give the authorization. If an elder has questions concerning a payroll check, he can ask either the bookkeeper or the elder who keeps the minutes. No two people on staff can get together and write a check for any reason.

Financial Record Keeping and Donor Lists

Generally, churches are expected to keep lists of people who donate funds and track the amounts they give. But such lists should be carefully guarded in light of Jesus' words in Matthew 6:3–4:

> But when you give alms, do not let your left hand know what your right hand is doing; that your alms may be in secret; and your Father who sees in secret will repay you.

The principle behind this instruction addresses the situation of some people knowing what others are giving. For example, if pastors or elders know that one person gives $10,000 to the church and another person only gives $50, it is difficult to treat both persons equally. Furthermore, James asks us to strictly guard ourselves from showing any partiality to the wealthier members of the Body (James 2:1–13) because of the sin of partiality introduced into the Body.

Therefore, choosing not to keep donor lists can produce positive spiritual growth for the Body. One church reports they carefully explain the reasoning behind their policy of not producing receipts for giving. They have discovered that donors appreciate this policy. In fact, many thank the church for keeping their giving anonymous. Some even thank the church because this policy has forced them to keep better records themselves.

Another area where the wisdom of this policy is evident concerns missionaries. Sometimes individuals want to give to a missionary on a one-time basis, but they definitely do not want to be placed on a mailing list or donor list. When the missionaries ask the church for a list of who gave, the church replies that it doesn't keep track and then goes on to explain why. It is often helpful to suggest to the missionaries that they put a general "thank you" note in the bulletin, which is directed at the whole Body. In this way, the people who give financially aren't singled out for special recognition over the ones who pray or support the ministry in other ways.

This policy prevents strong-minded persons from going to donors and putting pressure on them for continual support. Since nobody knows who the donors are, information about donations remains with the person who gave. This fits with the Scriptural view of giving mentioned above.

Designated Giving

Let's consider a very specific aspect of giving—how to handle designated funds. We include a policy statement written by an elder at one church, and adopted by several other churches.

Giving to Individuals — Is it possible to give money to worthy individuals by sending a check to the church and specifically designating the funds for that person?

The IRS Code does not allow giving specific monies to a specific individual and claiming the gift as a tax deduction. Passing the funds through a middle-man, like a nonprofit corporation, isn't allowable either. The nonprofit corporation jeopardizes its tax exempt status if it permits this kind of giving.

How then are we to solve the problem of giving to worthwhile ministries and still be good stewards of the funds God entrusts to us by minimizing taxes? There are three possible solutions.

1. We can give directly to the individual, but not claim a tax deduction. (The Lord may motivate us to give without receiving the maximum tax benefit.)

2. We may give funds to a nonprofit organization such as the church without specifically designating that 100 percent of the funds given must go to a worthy individual. The law allows us to give to an organization if we give up our right to require exactly how the funds are distributed. This gives the leadership the responsibility, under their Articles of Incorporation, of spending and/or distributing the funds as they see fit.

3. On special occasions, a nonprofit corporation such as the church can specifically set up a need fund for an individual who fits the church's charter definition of a needy person. That is, the directors of the organization (elders) put in their

minutes a declaration that such a fund has been arranged for the benefit of this individual. People may give to that fund with the knowledge that the organization will dispense the funds to that needy individual. In this case, the law allows the taxpayer to claim a legitimate deduction.

It is perfectly legitimate for a nonprofit organization to establish a ministry fund for an individual (in contrast to a need fund.) The test is whether 100 percent of the funds given to an individual's ministry fund wind up being given to the individual. If the organization retains funds to cover other types of expenses, like administration or insurance, then the taxpayer can claim a deduction.

It is always problematic when someone sends in a check and asks that all the money be given to an individual. Often we return the check to the donor and explain why we cannot pass it on. Depending on the circumstances, the elders may create a special fund to get money to the designated person. However, it is better to give the money directly to the person in need and not take a tax deduction, or contact the elders and ask them to consider setting up a fund to which individuals might give for helping the needy person.

Financial Reporting to the Body

A high priority for elders is the integrity of accurate financial bookkeeping and prompt, clear reporting to the local Body. One church asked us for help because they had not received a financial report from their accountant in four years. They had no idea what their current balance was or the state of their ministry accounts.

"He [the accountant] pays the bills when he gets around to it," they told me. "What about paying the staff?" I asked. "Oh, they get paid every two weeks, more or less." This was a church of more than 1,000 attendees!

My first task was to visit their accountant. I found him in the most cluttered office I have ever seen. Boxes stacked on top of boxes, tax returns in various stages lying haphazardly all over the place, a large desk piled high with reams of correspondence. Behind it all sat a white-haired gentleman with garters on his shirt sleeves and a green eye-shade on his forehead! He meant well, but this church needed a modernized accounting and reporting system.

We helped them establish a simple cash accounting procedure with a local bank. The statement used copies of the weekly giving deposit slips (coded for receipt accounts) as the income document and copies of checks written by a bookkeeper (coded for disbursement accounts) as the payables document. The bank then printed an operating statement each month from which a report was prepared and distributed to the congregation no later than two Sundays after the close of the month.

In addition, each month the bookkeeper balanced three important documents:

- The operating statement from the bank;
- The monthly bank statement
- The church check book

When all three documents were in balance, it was certain that no monies had been lost and all payments were accounted for.

On the next three pages, we include two reporting examples taken from different churches.

Figure 1 is a copy of an actual year-end report prepared for the local body, and based on the procedure we've just described. Figure 2 is a weekly financial report published in the Sunday bulletin, as a smaller church might do. We've used older examples to help preserve anonymity while maintaining authenticity.

FIGURE 1

Statement of Receipts Collected and Expenses Disbursed
For the Year Ended September 30, 1987

RECEIPTS
Undesignated Funds:

General Fund	$1,349,019	
Missions	6,264	
Interest	6,342	$1,361,625

Designated Funds:

Need	$12,756	
Weddings	1,442	
Food Cupboard	2,088	
Family Camp	25,704	
Men's Retreats	23,618	
Mexicali Outreach	18,470	
Ministries	48,155	
All Others	7,806	140,039

TOTAL GENERAL RECEIPTS $1,501,664

DISBURSEMENTS

Pastors' Salaries & Allowances	$665,793	
General Staff Salaries	252,172	
Employee Benefits	130,671	
Office Equipment	14,704	
Office Operating Items	46,578	
Plant Operating Items	109,924	
Travel Expenses	7,668	
College/High School Ministries	117,145	
Family Camp	26,543	
Men's Retreats	21,640	
Mexicali Outreach	16,726	
Honoraria	1,400	
Administration	692	
Missions Supported	10,467	
Special Funds—Food Cupboard	$1,070	
Need	9,189	
All Others	1,757	12,016

TOTAL GENERAL DISBURSEMENTS $1,434,139

NET RECEIPTS OVER DISBURSEMENTS $67,525

GRAND TOTALS OF OPERATIONS

Net Total For All Years Prior to 1973 = $ 3,838

	1973-84	1985	1986	1987
Grand Total Receipts	$7,670,390	$1,228,093	$1,374,282	$1,571,536
Grand Total Disbursements	$7,639,306	$1,281,139	$1,360,877	$1,553,818

NET FROM
TOTAL OPERATIONS $31,084   <$53,046> $13,405 $17,718

CURRENT NET TOTAL FOR ALL YEARS TO DATE: $12,999

< > Denotes negative balance

* * *

FIGURE 2

Financial Report	
Financial Report as of last week:	
Income for May:	$21,193
Income to date for June:	$18,062
Total average monthly expenses:	$17,150

On the weekly bulletin report (Figure 2) the line entitled "Total average monthly expense" is calculated this way:

Every six months the bookkeeper takes the previous six months of expense history and calculates an average monthly expense the church has experienced. This is done to give the congregation a weekly guideline of average expenses versus weekly and monthly giving. (For specific information by major accounts, the congregation receives the monthly statement.)

The advantages of this church accounting system are several. It presents sufficient information in a simple format for the congregation to make giving decisions, as the Spirit directs, without coercion. Also, by reviewing the past years' summaries at the bottom of the annual statement, the congregation can see how God has led through the years. The people in the Body are regularly informed, the financial information is easily understood, the system is concise and simple (reducing errors), and our Lord is honored.

CHAPTER ELEVEN

Elder Evaluation and Accountability

When the Spirit of God moves in a church, the enemy tries to move as well. The church leadership becomes a prime target of the enemy. Temptations are sure to come, and our adversary the devil is well aware of our individual weaknesses.

When a leader falls into a pattern of sin, the elder board's handling of the necessary confrontation and subsequent discipline is of utmost importance. The following example shows one church's struggle with moral failure among the leadership and the eventual path to repentance and restoration.

I was seated in my office when the phone rang. The caller introduced himself as a detective in the San Francisco police department. Thus began one of the strangest situations I've ever experienced as an elder.

"Do you know Phil Spalding*?" he asked. (Phil was an elder in our church.)

"Yes, why do you ask?"

"We are conducting an investigation for a fraud case."

Why is he interested in Phil? I wondered. So that evening I called Phil and told him about my conversation. He responded with this story:

"A short time ago my wallet was stolen when I was at lunch. Then the other day I was walking along a street in downtown San Francisco. The wind was blowing, and a piece of paper blew past me and up against a building. I picked it up and as I looked at it, there was my name. I couldn't believe it but, there it was. The rest of the paper had numbers and things I didn't understand, so I took the paper to the police. That must be why they are calling you."

As I listened, I thought, *This is bizarre.* When I asked Phil if there was anything I could do for him, he replied no, except to pray that everything would work out.

Several weeks went by and I heard from the detective again. He was interested in Phil's spending habits and anything that might reflect a recent change in his lifestyle.

While all this was going on, it happened that the elder evaluation schedule was brought up at the elders' meeting. To my surprise, Phil was the next one in line for evaluation.

Evaluation procedure

Our evaluation practice was based on 2 Corinthians 13:5:

Test yourselves to see if you are in the faith; examine yourselves! Or do you not recognize this about your-

*Note: Not his real name.

**selves, that Jesus Christ is in you—unless indeed you
fail the test?**

Whenever an elder's name came up for evaluation, two elders
were assigned to meet with him privately to discuss what was happening in three areas of his life. We asked questions regarding:

His family life

How is the elder doing with his wife in light of Ephesians
5:25–33? Is he loving her unselfishly as Christ did for the church?

How is it going with his children? How would he rate himself
according to Ephesians 6:4?

His occupational life

How is it going at work? Are his actions in harmony with
Ephesians 6:5–9? How is God using him in the marketplace?

His spiritual life

How is his walk with the Lord? What is God working on in
his life? Is the elder growing in his knowledge of the Word?"

Although the two elders assigned to this task were to ask penetrating questions, they were reminded to be gentle because their
evaluation would come up soon. Sometimes the team met with the
elder's wife; sometimes they asked the person to write a paper
addressing the three areas. The idea was to be flexible and trust the
Holy Spirit to adapt the process to fit the man.

Once the process was complete, they summarized their find-
ings and presented what they had learned to the full elder board.
This meeting included the elder being evaluated. Comments, clari-
fications, and questions continued until everyone understood the
information presented.

At this point, the person being evaluated would be excused
from the meeting. The other elders remained to seek the mind of
the Lord for His words for this person. Usually this process took

some time. Occasionally the issue of spiritual gifts came up. In the case of one pastor's evaluation, we asked, "Are we beginning to see that he doesn't have the necessary gifts to do what he has been asked to do in this church?" In another case of an elder's evaluation, we questioned, "Is his workload so demanding that he really doesn't have the time to function as an elder?"

Arriving at a unanimous decision for what God wants a person to hear is difficult. The process requires much thought and prayer. It's wise to put the conclusion in writing but unwise to simply send off a letter. The best approach is to have the same team of elders sit down privately with the person and lovingly share what the elders have decided unanimously.

Finally, the elder himself must come before the Lord with the results of an evaluation. This may mean reprioritizing his life. It may mean taking a leave of absence, or stepping down from being an elder or pastor. It is essential to remember that the Lord is in charge and He is responsible for His church.

But what about Phil?

It happened that I was selected as one of the two elders to talk with Phil. At first, he seemed comfortable and confident as we discussed the three areas of his life. But as time went on I sensed a nervousness and evasiveness in him. My colleague was likewise concerned.

One day a man in our congregation casually mentioned to me that he had lent Phil a large sum of money for a real estate deal. Later on I heard about another man who had lent Phil money for another seemingly worthwhile project. Soon I knew of half a dozen people to whom Phil owed significant sums of money.

When we questioned him, we got increasingly vague and irrational answers. Phil claimed to be a victim of a giant conspiracy involving his work, the police, friends, and neighbors.

The day came when it was time to confront him. It was a tough session. He made denials, accusations, and threats. Finally, the Spirit of God began to get through. At last, Phil acknowledged that he had extorted money from people in our congregation and at work for the purpose of keeping a mistress and taking expensive trips with her. His wife of some thirty years was completely ignorant of this. He had lived a double life for years until the Spirit of God began to bring it out in the open, using Phil's evaluation as part of the process.

Sadly, Phil did not turn from his sin right away. Instead, he left the country and lived in Europe with his mistress. But God didn't give up on him. Eventually, Phil repented and was reconciled to his long-suffering wife. He sold his home and cabin, and repaid all his debts. He and his wife decided to return to our church where he was accountable to an elder for a number of years. Now, after years of steady growth, he is even participating in the ministry again.

As I look back, I think of all the "it just so happens" and the "coincidences" which brought this hidden evil to light. I am so thankful that we were well established in conducting evaluations and that God had prepared His elders to face these serious matters.

How to confront a sinning leader

Having a ministry in the San Francisco area is not without its hazards. Another crisis in our Bay-area church occurred when a spiritual leader began to invite young men to join him in his private sauna. Rumors began to circulate through the congregation. When the elders heard of it, first one, then two went to this leader to confront him. After they were able to verify the behavior, they urged him to renounce his sinful activities. Nothing seemed to change even after an elder wrote the following letter.*

---

*Letter used by permission.

Dear Richard,

I am not sure what to say to you in this letter but I feel strongly compelled to write you and try to express what is on my heart. I beg you to read it through with the realization that it comes from one who loves you and feels deeply pained at what appears to be certain spiritual (if not mortal) disaster into which you are heading.

Information has reached me this week of the homosexual involvement which you and Dick Sims* have had with Sam Jones* and also with several other young men from South Hills Community Church. [The elder writing the letter then specifically listed the charges, which we have deleted here due to their necessarily graphic nature.]

Richard, you have admitted to Fred Brooks that this behavior is wrong and un-Christian, yet you continue to get involved in these episodes and to defend them as manifestations of Christian love. It is bad enough that these homosexual acts are hurtful to you. By your own admission I think the experience of the last two years has given all who know you ample evidence of the truth of Romans 1:27, "Men committing shameless acts with men and receiving in their own person the due penalty for their error."

But what is far worse is that you and Sims are both actively ensnaring other young men in the sexual trap and doing so in the name of Christian love! Beyond actual homosexuality you have been encouraging young men to indulge in premarital sex and even to habitually sleep with their girlfriends and consider themselves "married" in doing so. Sam Jones is a case in point. How you can do such things in the face of the solemn words of the Lord Himself, I do not know. He said: "Temptations to sin are sure to come; but woe to him by whom they come! It would be better for him if a millstone were hung round his neck and he were cast into the sea, than that he should cause one of these little ones to sin."

*The names have been changed.

I do not say this self-righteously. The Lord knows I have been guilty of causing others to sin and may do so again, but by God's grace I do not want to defend such action or in anyway justify it. I know God is no respecter of persons and I have no desire to face His righteous anger in such instances. The only escape you or I have is in full and complete acknowledgment of the evil and a determination to forsake it by God's power and never justify it under any circumstances.

Richard, either you have power from the Lord to forsake these practices once and for all or you don't. If you do, and don't choose to use this power, then you have only yourself to blame—no one else. If you don't have such power, then either you are not a Christian at all (which I doubt) or the promises of God are not true and Christianity is nothing but a big hoax (which I don't believe). Which is it?

My own conviction is that your pride has never permitted you to make a full and complete renunciation of these acts as sinful and wicked. Therefore you have never been free from their enslaving power. You go back to them again and again because you have not clearly and publicly confessed them as wrong. You have kept on making provision for the flesh to fulfill the lust, and that is why you cannot break these chains. Dick Sims has been of no help to you at all in this, nor have you been to him, and that damnable sauna has been an open doorway to temptation, which you have refused to close.

I do not know how many more chances you have left. But I do know that as far as the Body of Christ at our church and South Hills is concerned, there is nothing left for us to do but to take the step enjoined in Matthew 18 and "tell it to the church." What is meant by the phrase "to deliver one to Satan for the destruction of the flesh, that the spirit may be saved in the day of the Lord Jesus" (1 Timothy 1:20) is not clear to me, but I know that it is something done out of love and for the ultimate benefit of the one so delivered.

Richard, with all my heart I believe that you are in grave spiritual danger. Your heart is being hardened and bitterness and hate possess your soul. You are being destroyed by Satan and there is no escape unless you genuinely and thoroughly repent.

Because you have done grave and repeated harm to the Body of Christ I personally believe that any such repentance should be in the form of a public confession to the Body, and a public renunciation of your sin. Your brothers and sisters are more than eager to receive such a confession and to help you abundantly to escape this evil.

But time is running out. It is likely that a public announcement of this situation will be made in both churches on Sunday, March 23. If I have not heard from you by Thursday, March 20, such an announcement will be made. No Christian Body can be expected to stand by and watch youth being destroyed in the name of Christianity, and not make a vigorous protest and take what action they can to minimize the danger.

So I plead with you Richard, in the name of all that's holy, and out of remembrance of those happier days when God used you in great power in many ways—stop! Listen! Give heed! "It is a fearful thing to fall into the hands of the Living God."

Faithfully in Christ,

When the letter received no response, we had no choice but to engage in the painful process of church discipline. After long hours of discussion and prayer the elders reached a unanimous decision to proceed with the Lord's directions in Matthew 18:15. We had already accomplished steps one and two a number of times, as different individuals and groups had approached Richard. We chose a Sunday on which to make this grave announcement to the church Body and sent Richard a registered letter indicating our decision.

Just before the day we received a registered letter back from Richard threatening to sue us if we mentioned his name in public.

Without hesitation the elders proceeded, asking Dave Roper to teach on Matthew 18.

Here is a portion of that message, along with questions that were asked by members of the congregation. This message was given at a Body Life service at Peninsula Bible Church on March 23, 1975, to accomplish discipline in line with the teaching of Jesus in Matthew 18. In all the years that PBC has been in existence, this kind of action has occurred only twice.

We make this teaching available to the Body-at-large so that you might see how our church handled a very difficult problem. We hope that his example will not be taken out of context or used inappropriately. We trust our readers to consider the truth presented here. All comments and questions at the end were from members of the congregation. All the answers were by David Roper.

It is difficult to convey the amount of prayer, discussion, and careful thought that preceded this action over a period of two years.

If Your Brother Sins Against You . . .

Believe me, there are about a hundred things I would rather do tonight than what I have to do now. As you know, the New Testament gives us very clear directives about the way we're to treat brothers and sisters in Christ who act contrary to Scripture.

In Matthew 18, the Lord gives us some instruction concerning the specific approach we are to take with a brother or sister who is violating clearly stated commands in Scripture. This does not concern violation of conscience, but rather a violation of principles or commands in Scripture that are clearly stated and about which there is no question. When a brother or sister is living contrary to the truth there are certain things that are to be done and they must be done in a spirit of love.

Jesus said in Matthew 18:15:

> **If your brother sins against you, go and tell him his fault, between you and him alone. If he listens to you, you have gained your brother. But if he does not listen, take one or two others along with you, that every word may be confirmed by two or three witness. If he refuses to listen to them, tell it to the church: and if he refuses to listen even to the church, let him be to you as a Gentile and a tax collector.**

These are weighty words. Jesus said that if we see a brother or sister overtaken in a fault or participating in some sin, we're not to gossip behind their backs, nor are we to turn our backs on them. We're not to reject them; we're not to ostracize them; nor are we to overlook their sin. We're to go to them, first in private, and point out to them the specific area of disobedience.

Paul gives us a further note on this practice in Galatians 6. He says that we're to go in a spirit of meekness, considering ourselves lest we also be tempted, recognizing that we're all prone to fall into sin. At one time I may be the brother you have to approach, and another time you may be the brother or sister I have to approach. It works both ways. None of us has the right merely to sit in judgment on another brother without being willing to have that brother come to us in love and point out some area of sin in our life.

And yet if we see a brother who is sinning, we're to go to that person and between the two of us we're to sit down and look at what the Scriptures have to say on that issue, and to do so in a loving and gentle spirit. Then, if he refuses to hear the truth, we're to take two or three more to speak with him about the matter.

This is not a pressure tactic to try to force him to respond. Rather, we need to show him that this is not a personal vendetta on the part of one individual but something that affects the entire Body. In the same spirit of love and gentleness, approach and talk with him.

Jesus said that if he still won't respond, if he won't repent and forsake that sin, we are then to tell it to the church, not, however, in a condemning way.

The purpose of this action is constructive and redemptive. The hope is that other members of the Body who know that individual will go to him and appeal to him to return to the Lord and that all will pray for that brother. Then Jesus said if he still would not respond we're to treat him as a tax collector and a sinner.

That has often been taken as justification for making an outcast out of a sinning brother, throwing him out of the church, ostracizing him or excommunicating him. But that's not what Jesus meant. If you know anything of the heart of our Lord, you know how he treated tax collectors and sinners. He loved them and ministered to them, but he treated them as those outside the family, outside the people of God.

Jesus' point is that if a person who calls himself a Christian can resist the kind of loving treatment he outlines here, this gentle handling over a long period of time, then he must not in fact be a Christian. Anyone who has Christ in his heart cannot hold out against that kind of approach. So, if our brother rejects the truth after his sin has been announced to the church, then he is to be treated as an unbeliever.

In 1 and 2 Corinthians we have a New Testament illustration of the procedure in practice. In 1 Corinthians we learn that there was a brother in Corinth who was guilty of flagrant sin, and he was corrected in the way Jesus had described it should be done. Then in 2 Corinthians we have an added note that indicates that the brother repented and came back to the Lord and to the Body. Paul says that since this happened, this brother is to be received warmly and welcomed back into fellowship because, Paul says, "We're not ignorant of Satan's devices" (2 Corinthians 2:11). His point is that Satan can cause us to have a critical, unforgiving spirit and reject that brother because of some sin he's committed, and refusing to receive him back would bring about a split among the Body there.

The thing that I want to underscore in all of this is that this action is redemptive; it's constructive. This is no ultimate condemnation; it's designed to bring a brother back. By and large, the church has forsaken this practice because we're afraid of it. But it is clearly spelled out in Scripture, and we cannot avoid it.

Therefore, in line with these instructions, and with deep regret, we announce that our brother and friend Richard Seafair has for some months now been engaging in homosexual acts with young men. We're certain of this; there's no question—the evidence is overwhelming. He has been approached on numerous occasions by one, and then by two or three or more. He has been appealed to, to repent and forsake his sin. In certain situations where he could not deny the facts he has admitted that he has done these things and he has named them as sin—he knows he is guilty of wrongdoing—but he later justifies them and is unwilling to forsake them.

Therefore, for his sake and for the sake of those young men over whom he has influence, we feel we must tell it to the church. We do this with a great deal of personal sorrow, and this is certainly not a precipitous action. We've weighed and pondered this decision for a number of months. He has been appealed to many times, and much prayer and thought and effort have been put into securing his repentance, but since he doesn't seem disposed to respond, we feel we can wait no longer.

I want to say again that we are not doing this in a vindictive way. All of us recognize our own weakness and any of us could fall into even graver sin, given the right circumstances. We recognize our own need for repentance and forgiveness and, but for God's grace, we would all be in a similar situation. So, far from reflecting a judgmental attitude, this is an attempt again to reach out to him in love and have him return to fellowship with this Body.

This man is a good friend of mine and of many of you here in the congregation, and this is exceedingly difficult for me. I'm sure that some of you have come to Christ because of his influence in the past. We appeal to you as his friends and members of the Body of Christ to pray for him and if you know him, to correspond with him and to appeal to him to forsake this sin and return to the Lord. We believe that the Lord will grant to him forgiveness, and may grant to him a more fruitful ministry in years to come.

Question: How do we decide that certain sins are to be brought to the attention of the church while others are not?

Answer: This is an excellent question, because as a matter of fact there are sins that from the point of view of Scripture appear to result in far greater damage than the sin of which this person is guilty. David, for instance, was much more severely disciplined for his pride on the occasion when he numbered Israel and took pride in the size of his army than for his sins of adultery and murder.

Whenever a brother is guilty of gossip or a divisive spirit, or bears resentment against his parents or some other person and he persists in that sin and refuses to respond, the same procedure ought to be followed. And we've done that. We don't always do it consistently and that's to our shame, but we have tried to follow up on these things. There are many of you here, individual believers, who have talked at various times with different brothers, and their response was to repent. When that happens the matter is ended. Jesus says in the very next paragraph after this section in Matthew 18 that if your brother sins against you and he repents, you must forgive him 490 times. It does not need to go any farther. If he repents then it's all over and the relationship is restored. Ninety-nine percent of the time it never goes any farther than that, but in those cases where it does, regardless of the type of sin, it ought to be handled in this way. We're not singling out sexual sin as particularly heinous. All sin is damaging, and thus abhorrent.

Question: Is it necessary to make public the name of the brother whose sin you are announcing to the church?

Answer: Yes. Scripture is very specific about these things. Paul wrote the whole epistle of Philippians to the church in Philippi because of two ladies who were causing problems in the church. They couldn't get along; they had been appealed to many times, but they kept on fighting and getting everybody upset, so Paul wrote this letter to the church. He lays down an awful lot of theology before he gets to the personal issue—it's all about the unity of the Body and how to preserve that unity through a spirit of humility and willingness to give up one's rights. In order to understand the impact of this you have to realize that these letters were read in public, as they only had the one scroll. Then, as the reader came to the end of the letter, with the entire congregation listening attentively, he read, "I beseech you Euodia and Syntyche to agree in the Lord." He named them. If we didn't name the person, there would be a great deal of speculation, since we all know people who are struggling with various sins. It's necessary to name him, also, so you can go to that brother and continue to appeal to him. If you don't know who he is, you can't do that.

As to the young men who were involved with Richard, the Scripture says clearly that what they're doing is wrong and destructive, and in most cases they know that and they've turned away from it. In fact, this is how we know some of the circumstances. These men have come to us and have admitted wrongdoing and have asked for help, and Scripture looks at them as it looks at anyone else who sins and turns away from it—they're forgiven. The blood of Jesus Christ covers and cleanses us from all sin—all sin, not just certain kinds of sin.

Question: Was Mr. Seafair informed that this announcement would be made?

Answer: He was informed and correspondence was sent, so he was fully aware of our intent. He was told, also, that we would retract instantly if he would come and talk to us and would be willing to turn away before the announcement was made. This announcement was made simultaneously at another church, which was directly involved, and we kept the lines open so that we could phone them immediately if we were contacted by this person.

Question: How much of a factor is Richard's position of influence as a teacher in deciding at what point one goes to the whole Body?

Answer: The Scriptures say that a leader is to be rebuked before all because his influence is so widespread (1 Timothy 5:20), and that did have bearing on our decision. It is true that leaders have far greater responsibility and great culpability. That's a heavy one for all of us. That's why we read in James, "Let not many of you become teachers, my brethren, for you know that we who teach shall be judged with greater strictness" (James 3:1).

Comment: I've had contact with Richard Seafair over the last three or four months, probably more than most here, and I've been a friend of his for ten years. He led my wife to the Lord, and we've traveled all over the country ministering together. There's no human being that I love more and yet I've told him personally that the evidence was overwhelming and that this move was necessary. When you really see what sin does to the mind of somebody you love, the tragic effects it has and the crumbling into weakness, it's very hard to bear. The key thing here is, as Paul says, when something comes to the light it becomes light. When our will has hardened in response to the Spirit of God, we need additional light—opportunity, if you like—to respond to God. And I think that this is the final act of another level of hope, another level where Richard can experience all of your prayers and your correspondence and the evidence that your life is at stake with his life. This is what God wants to come out of it, and He does want Richard restored. As one who loves him very dearly, I was foremost in voting that we should do this, and I hope it will bring the right results.

Comment: I think as an act of love, since this is a Body ministry, we ought to be very careful what we say to the world outside regarding this matter. I don't think it would be edifying to Mr. Seafair for us to go back to our school and job situations and say, "Hey, guess what we did Sunday night at church?" This is a Body ministry; judgment begins in the household of God. This is a concern of Christians—we don't want to set Richard up to be mocked by the world. That's not the function. So I think this is something we ought to confine to the Body of Christ. I think all of us when we pray for Richard tonight ought to make ourselves available to God to be used in his life.

Question: How do we ensure that legalism doesn't creep into our Body—that's death, too. I can't see how we balance, how we can be sure that we're not witch-hunting.

Answer: I think the thing that will keep our action positive is the motivation behind it. Why do we do it? Our concern is love. Our concern is not to get Richard or anyone else to measure up to some arbitrary standards that we set forth. We know that violation of God's law will ultimately destroy a man—"for the wages of sin is death"—and our concern is for Richard and his soul and his life. As long as we continue to operate in that way, out of love and out of concern for the man, then I think we can guard against legalism.

Restoration!

Five years went by during which Richard was estranged from the Lord and our congregation. I remember entering a restaurant for lunch one day and saw him seated by himself in a corner. I went over to greet him and as I approached he looked up, recognized me, and then turned his face to the wall, refusing to speak or acknowledge me in any way. I remember his appearance: puffy face and red-veined nose, bags under red-rimmed eyes, soiled clothes, all giving the appearance of someone about to end up in the gutter. I remember a great feeling of sadness and loss—this man had been in our home and we had shared the same platform in ministry.

Could God still rescue him?

Here is the letter* he wrote when he finally came to the end of himself:

My fellow Christians,

> *Several years ago the congregations of PBC and South Hills Community Church took public action against me in accordance with Matthew 18:15–20. The charges against me were true.*

> *I cannot reverse history and relive the events that led up to my downfall. I have harmed many people and brought ruin to myself. Because I was an outspoken, prominent member of the Christian community my sins have been all the more deplorable and horrendous.*

> *After I became a Christian some eighteen years ago I failed to deal thoroughly with lust, covetousness, and masturbation. In time I became self-deceived, proud, and arrogant. Moreover, eventually God shouted upon the housetops that which I had tried desperately to keep hidden. God finally let me go into alcoholism and sexual immorality, both of which were worse than I experienced before my conversion. Twice I went through the horror and hell of manic-depressive psychoses (as Nebuchadnezzar did) that I might learn that God resists the proud but gives grace to the humble.*

> *I am very fortunate to be alive. I came very close to suicide and should have died in ignominy and disgrace except for the Scripture*

*Letter used by permission.

which says, "Wilt Thou perform wonders for the dead? Will the departed spirits rise and praise Thee? Will Thy lovingkindness be declared in the grave, or Thy faithfulness in Abaddon?"

I am in need of your forgiveness for I have wronged you all. I earnestly desire your prayers for wholeness and complete deliverance from homosexuality. The church widely believes today that there is no cure for homosexuality beyond arrested development as a celibate. I am certain that God can do much more than he has already done for me and for countless others in this area who are afflicted with this crippling disease.

It is impossible for me to retrace my footsteps and right every wrong, however I welcome the opportunity to meet and pray with any individuals who have something against me that needs resolution. I am looking and waiting for the further grace and mercy of God in this matter. What you have bound on earth has been bound in heaven and I now know your actions were done in love for my own good and that of the Body of Christ.

Sincerely,

Richard Seafair

God began to restore "the years the locusts had eaten," as Joel 2:25 says. It took time. For two years a godly brother met each week with Richard, helping him back to spiritual health. Gradually God restored his ministry and once more he is a frequent guest in my home.

God is faithful!

APPENDIX I

Questions and Answers

Here are twenty-five common questions about elders and their ministry in the local church.

Question: How do we select elders when starting a church, or adopting an elder form of government?

Answer: Scripture says that the Holy Spirit selects elders (Acts 20:28). While the apostle Paul charged Titus with appointing elders in every city they had visited on the island of Crete, there are no such apostolic messengers today. We must be wise about providing the means by which the Holy Spirit will select His men to serve as elders.

Eldership is based on the spiritual character qualities and gifts as defined in 1 Timothy 3, Titus 1, Ephesians 4 and 1 Corinthians

12–14. Hence, it seems prudent that we begin by looking for men whom God has already matured in terms of spiritual character and who already have begun to display the required spiritual gifts given to them by the Holy Spirit.

If the Lord is in charge of His church and the Holy Spirit apportions spiritual gifts to whomever He will (1 Corinthians 12), then it's only logical that the Lord will have men in the church whom He wants to be elders. The Spirit, who does all things to glorify the Lord Jesus, will have already assigned the necessary gifts to those men. Because of their mature Christian character, they will already have begun putting those gifts into practice. All we have to do is look around us for evidence of the necessary spiritual gifts at work.

Since God has already announced that this is the way He wishes to govern His church, if one cannot find men with the spiritual character who have the required spiritual gifts, then one should conclude that the Lord is not ready to start a church at this time, no matter what we think or want. Scripture indicates that there needs to be a plurality of elders, which mandates the Lord putting in place several men who can qualify. All the church-planting group needs to do is look around them with the Scriptural criteria in mind, and ask the Lord of the Church to show them the men He has already selected. In the end, it should be clear who the prospective elders are.

To whom are the sheep already responding for leadership and teaching? Who is already out there among the sheep ministering with the qualifications and gifts Paul speaks of in 1 Corinthians 12–14, Ephesians 4, and in 1 Timothy and Titus? Our task is to recognize those God has already appointed.

Elders must never be self-appointed or selected in a cavalier way by slapping the title "elder" on a few men who are committed to start a new work or adopt the eldership form of government. It is natural when starting a new work for God to use many different folks with great hearts and proven gifts to establish that work, but only a few of the men will be called out by the Holy Spirit to become elders for the long term. We must all have a healthy respect for this fact: the Holy Spirit alone makes and selects elders in the local church.

Question: How many elders are too few, or too many?

Answer: There are no obvious guidelines on this, but it is apparent that no church in the New Testament was ever served by a lone elder. Titus was charged by Paul to "appoint elders in every city" (Titus 1:5) on the island of Crete. We suggest that there ought to be more than two, since the dominant personality may prevail over the quieter man.

As to the maximum number, having more than fifteen elders could become unwieldy and create a belabored process to solicit every man's opinion before the Lord. So as a general guideline, the minimum might be three, and the maximum might be fifteen.

Question: In most Brethren communities, there are no clergymen. But you talk freely about having elders and pastors serving simultaneously. What is the biblical justification for this?

Answer: There are really three primary biblical justifications for this. First, there is the spiritual gift of pastor-teacher, clearly outlined by Paul as a foundation of a local church in Ephesians 4:11. The pastor-teacher is to equip the Body of Christ for the work of the ministry. By itself, this passage fails to justify the existence of pastors in the local church. The word for pastor here is *poïmen,* translated elsewhere in its verbal form as "to shepherd" and applied contextually to elders (see Acts 20:28).

Second, there are many passages which identify elders as the primary governing body in the local church. They include Acts 15; Acts 20:17–38; 1 Timothy 3 and 5; Titus 1; James 5:13–20; and 1 Peter 5.

Third, the letters of 1 and 2 Timothy present a local church situation where a younger man serves in a pastoral role without being an elder. Yet he serves alongside the very group of elders Paul addressed in Acts 20. Timothy was never called an elder, yet he was called to be a pastor-teacher by preaching and teaching the Word and by confronting false teachers and errant doctrines. At the same time he was enjoined to appeal to the older men in the Body as fathers—as a pastor should respectfully approach the elders in the church. Thus, there is solid biblical basis for elders and pastors serving together in the local Body of believers.

F. F. Bruce's treatment of this in his book, *Answers to Questions,* is helpful. Bruce, one of the outstanding New Testament scholars of the 20th century, was a lifelong layman in the Plymouth Brethren movement. His book handles the question like this:

> Q: What is wrong with having a full-time pastor in the Scriptural sense of that word?
>
> A: There is nothing wrong with it. A full-time pastor is as scripturally justified as a full-time evangelist; and many local churches are spiritually declining for lack of adequate pastoral ministry.

Question: What should an elder's term of service be? Three years? For life? And should there be a sabbatical policy for elders?

Answer: The Scriptures do not prescribe any specific term for elders. However, we know that the Holy Spirit makes men elders in the local church, both by gifting and by calling. And we know from the text that the gifts and calling of God are irrevocable.

A man might disqualify himself by falling into immorality, or by some other character failing as outlined in 1 Timothy 3 and Titus 1. But it appears that an elder is an elder for life, as long as he continues to meet the character qualifications.

But elders are also men of clay, and thus a sabbatical policy is a good idea. A man might serve on the elder team for three to five years and then take a year off. Occasionally an elder's personal or home life may require that he take a sabbatical year to focus on the difficulties before him, or his fellow elders can help him tackle such issues as they arise.

Question: Speaking about an elder's qualification, what happens in the event that one of the elder's children rebels or leaves the faith?

Answer: In 1 Timothy 3:4–5, one of the qualifications of an elder is that he "manages his own household well, keeping his children under control with all dignity." Similarly, in Titus 1:6 an elder is one "having children who believe."

The key word in both of those passages is the word "children." The man must be bringing up his children in the fear and admonition of the Lord, teaching them the Scriptures, teaching them to pray, and loving them enough to discipline them without harshness. If a child under the elder's care is rebelling at a young age, or is declaring himself an atheist or agnostic while in junior high, then there would be cause to question the elder's qualification.

But as the child becomes an adult, we must consider the independent choices of these young men and women. Some of the best elders have offspring who walk away from the faith in early adulthood. I know of an elder who offered to resign because one of his daughters had rebelled. But the other elders refused to accept his resignation because she was an adult, making her own decisions, over which the elder could no longer exert control. The time of his direct responsibility was past, and he continued to serve as an elder.

Question: How do elders confront false teachers or misguided theology within the local Body?

Answer: Elders are to confront false teachers or propagators of misguided theology in the same way Paul enjoined Timothy in 2 Timothy 2:24–25:

And the Lord's bond-servant must not be quarrelsome, but be kind to all, able to teach, patient when
wronged, with gentleness correcting those who are in
opposition, if perhaps God may grant them repentance
leading to the knowledge of the truth.

One godly group of elders had to confront younger pastor-
teachers whose positions no longer reflected the church's doctrinal
statement. First, the elders confronted the men when they taught
publicly a doctrine which was contrary to the doctrinal statement.
The young pastor-teachers were then enjoined to study the issue
further on their own, and the entire pastoral staff embarked on a
yearlong Scriptural study that spoke eloquently to the issue.

This is a classic example of hard-minded but soft-hearted shepherding by elders—the issue of biblical truth and error was met
head-on by hard-minded elders, and the young pastor-teachers
were handled with soft-hearted graciousness in the hope that they
would come around and the doctrinal solidarity of the church
would be maintained.

Question: What about church discipline in an elder-led church?

Answer: Any elder-led church must adhere closely to the intent of
Scripture, since it is our eldership handbook. The Scriptures are
clear in Matthew 18 and 1 Corinthians 5 that church discipline
must be followed in the case of sin in the Body that soils the name
of Christ in the community. What is at stake is the moral heart of
the local Body, which is charged with reflecting the balanced
morality and integrity of Jesus Christ in the community.

When the apostle Paul addressed the Corinthian Christians
in 1 Corinthians 5, he called upon them to discipline the man
sleeping with his father's wife because even the debauched
Corinthians would have seen such a thing as immoral. Paul was
aghast that the elders were allowing such behavior to continue

unchecked in an area where even the immoral Corinthian unbelievers drew the line.

Today, we too must draw moral lines and invoke biblical church discipline if we are to have any hope of being salt and light in an increasingly wicked world.

Here are a few guidelines. First, allow a significant period of time after the person committing the sin was confronted privately. He or she should be confronted first by one individual, then by two, or even more—followed by a time of prayer for the offender to repent on his or her own.

Second, the sin must be obvious to everyone—if it requires too much explanation or even justification as to why discipline is necessary, then public discipline probably should be avoided.

Third, church discipline is all about restoration and bringing a brother or sister redemptively into the loving arms of Christ. It cannot degenerate into retribution or a personal vendetta against the offender.

If an elder is looking forward to the discipline, or is self-righteous when talking about the person, then he needs to prayerfully ask the Lord to search his heart, making sure the Spirit is motivating the disciplinary action, and that all is done redemptively with love as the primary motivation. (For more on this subject, consider chapter 9.)

Question: How often should elders meet?

Answer: There is no correct answer that will fit every case. Each team of elders must follow the Spirit in setting their meetings, both in the number of meetings per month and in determining the agenda for each meeting.

In a well-established elder-led church, meeting twice a month may be adequate. The strength of this approach is that each elder has time to pray and listen to the Lord in the two-week interval. In churches where the elder team is younger or the church less well-established, weekly meetings may be helpful.

One elder team meets every Tuesday, but at alternate times each week. On the first and third week, they meet at 6:15 a.m. This meeting is devoted to studying the Scriptures together. On the second and fourth week, they meet at 6:30 p.m. This meeting is discussion and decision oriented. This is how the Spirit led that group of men in their setting.

Question: How does an elder's life prior to becoming a Christian affect his qualification for eldership?

Answer: An elder's past, as an unregenerate man, has no bearing on his spiritual qualification for eldership once he has been regenerated by the indwelling Spirit. Second Corinthians 5:17 is helpful:

> **Therefore if any man is in Christ, he is a new creature; the old things have passed away; behold, new things have come.**

If the old things have passed away, there is no reason to dig them up.

Question: More pointedly, can a man become an elder if he has been divorced when he was a believer?

Answer: This is a more difficult question. In both 1 Timothy 3 and Titus 1, the list of qualifications begins similarly: the man "must be above reproach, the husband of one wife."

There are two basic interpretations of this. Some scholars say that "husband of one wife" means he is currently married to only one woman, regardless of his past. Other scholars say it means he has never been married to more than one woman.

But the text seems very clear. The verb "be" in both cases is in the present tense—he must currently be the husband of one wife. If he could never have been divorced or married to a woman who has died, it seems that the qualification would read, "He must always have been the husband of one wife."

The heart of this principle is that the man must be a "one-woman man," without a roving eye that makes him vulnerable to adultery. The elder must demonstrate fidelity in his marriage. If he is fickle here, he will be unfaithful in leading the church.

If the man is faithfully married now, but has a former wife and significant child-care responsibilities from a past marriage, then his parental responsibilities may be too many and too varied to allow him to serve effectively as an elder. If he is currently faithfully married, and his divorce happened many years ago and has virtually no bearing on his current situation, then he could qualify. If he is currently faithfully married, but was divorced due to his own infidelity, then the elders need to delve more deeply.

The key is "currently faithfully married," implying that he has dealt spiritually with marital mistakes of the past and is currently trusting in God's presence and power for his current marriage.

Question: Speaking of qualifications, what does "apt to teach or able to teach" mean?

Answer: In 1 Timothy 3:2, one of the qualifications is "apt to teach or able to teach," depending on the translation. This means that each elder must have a desire to teach the Word of God in some setting in the church—whether in the pulpit for those with a strong preaching or teaching gift, in a Sunday school class, in a home fellowship, or in a small group discipleship setting.

Any man who is not able to teach because of a lack of desire or giftedness ought not to serve as an elder, because a critical task of the shepherd is to make sure the sheep are fed. The Lord is clearly concerned about starving the sheep and therefore says this spiritual gift is necessary for those qualifying to govern His church.

Question: What are the most often observed failures on the part of the elders?

Answer: There are seven common pitfalls for elders.

1. Elders can become men of ego rather than men of prayer. Satan's strategy when tempting Jesus was to try to get Jesus to prove He was the Son of God. Two of the three temptations started with "If you are the Son of God . . . ," thus taunting Him to prove Himself (Matthew 4:3,6). If elders begin to see themselves as the head of the local church, then they can easily be caught by the snare of pride. If they see themselves as brothers on a quest to discern the mind of the Lord Jesus who is head of the church, then they can avoid this pitfall.

2. Elders can be tripped up by succumbing to time pressure to make a hasty decision. Hasty decisions are nearly always authored by the evil one or the flesh, not the Spirit.

3. Conversely, elders can invite years of heartache and unnecessary struggle by failing to confront a difficult issue or a problem person in a timely manner. When the elders are reticent to speak to a tough issue or person, the problem does not go away—it festers and worsens.

4. Elders can easily fall into the trap of failing to speak up "because I don't know enough." If the Holy Spirit has appointed a man to be an elder through the unanimous decision of the existing elders, then He has equipped him with what he needs to speak to an issue, even if it is to share a vague lack of peace about something or to admit that he needs more time to study and pray over the issue. Not speaking up is sin.

5. In this day of frenetic activity, an elder may be too busy to minister effectively. If he is too busy to meet consistently with the other elders, or if he is too busy to faithfully shepherd a ministry to which he has been assigned, then he is too busy to be an elder. Unfortunately, the busiest elders may be the most gifted. But even the most gifted elder is of no value when he is absent.

By definition, biblical eldership requires consistent presence, as well as character qualifications and appointment by the Holy Spirit.

6. An elder may struggle with a crippling sense of personal inadequacy, focusing too much on himself rather than the Lord working through him. If this tendency plagues one man, and the entire group is seeking unanimity, then his failure can infect the entire elder team. This self-focus is sin.

7. Elders can revert to worldly solutions for tough issues, especially when problems drag out and the elders get so frustrated they will accept almost any solution. The Lord's timetable is not our timetable, and His solutions are often long in coming. Elders must be patient seekers after the mind of Christ.

Question: What will keep elders from getting off track?

Answer: So much is said about accountability groups and increased personal discipline in Bible study and prayer as the key to keeping us on track. But the Holy Spirit alone is able to keep elders from leaving the path. When elders quit listening to Him in any part of the process of shepherding, they have already begun to step off the track. Each man is accountable to his Lord to be walking in intimacy with the Spirit. God doesn't expect elders to be perfect but to be engaged with Him and listening to Him.

A regular review schedule is helpful here, where each man's relationship with his Lord, his wife, his children, his occupational responsibilities, his ministry team, and his sheep is evaluated, as well as his ongoing character qualifications to be an elder.

Question: How do elders avoid seeing themselves as the head over the local church they serve?

Answer: This subtle error creeps in easily. Elders must continually submit themselves to the authority of the Word of God and study the Word together. Jesus Christ alone is the head of the church universal, as well as the local church. The elders must see themselves as brothers united in a common quest—to find the mind of Christ, the only true head.

Question: What are the key biblical passages underlying the concept of eldership? What passages should we study to understand God's instructions to elders?

Answer: Here is a list of 16 relevant passages to study, followed by general titles of the areas covered by that passage:

Numbers 11:1–30 — elders in the wilderness: the Spirit is required;

Ruth — Boaz' submission to the local elders;

1 & 2 Kings — importance of the heart: as leadership goes, so goes the church;

Ezekiel 14, 34 — idolatry in elders' hearts, and a portrait of false elders (shepherds);

Mark 10:32–35 — definitional passage on eldering as servant-leadership;

John 21:15–17 — shepherding responsibilities;

Acts 15 — Council of Jerusalem: importance of unanimity;

Acts 20:17–38 — Paul's personal model of an elder's ministry;

1 Corinthians 1–3 — avoiding factionalism by finding the mind of Christ;

1 Timothy 3 — character qualities of an elder;

1 Timothy 5 — ministry/discipline of an elder;

Titus 1 — character qualities of an elder, justification of elders in every church;

James 5:13–20 — praying and confronting ministry of elders;

1 Peter 5 — calling of an elder;

3 John — the mindset of an elder: elder leadership in action;

Revelation 2, 3 — Jesus Christ as sovereign Lord of the churches.

Question: How should a moderator be chosen to chair the meetings?

Answer: To avoid any man having too much influence over the agenda and flow of the elder meetings, moderators should be chosen on a rotating basis, with each rotation lasting no longer than one year. This will ensure that all the elders will moderate the meetings eventually. Some men may be bad moderators, letting discussions go on without reaching the decision point, or forcing bottom-line decisions too quickly. In these cases, common sense dictates the moderator's term.

Question: Is it necessary to keep an agenda and minutes of the elder meetings?

Answer: In most states it is a legal requirement. A nonprofit corporation must have an annual business meeting of the directors, who in the case of an elder-led church are the elders. At the annual meeting of the corporation, officers should be chosen from the elders for the next year, and a motion should be carried that recognizes the minutes of the elder meetings throughout the year as the official record of the decisions of the directors of the corporation. This keeps the elders' decisions tied to the corporate entity.

Question: Is there any age when a man becomes "old enough" to be an elder?

Answer: Age doesn't seem to be an issue in the scriptural qualifications, although the term for "youthfulness" in 1 Timothy 4:12 is a Greek term meaning "under forty." It seems that any man under forty in that culture would have been considered youthful.

Without making any hard and fast rules, here are some observations. Generally speaking, no man in his early twenties should be considered an elder. A man in his late twenties or early thirties may be an elder when older, more mature men are on the board to balance out his youthful zeal.

Any man who has small children at home may simply be too busy to be an effective elder. He may end up sacrificing his time as a father to be an elder.

The key thing is whether the man has a proven track record in the church, so that hands are not laid on him too early, and that he meets the character qualifications set out in 1 Timothy 3 and Titus 1.

Question: Can women be elders?

Answer: Not according to the biblical ideal. There is no record of any woman who is called an elder in either the Hebrew Scriptures or the New Testament. Jesus Christ, who disregarded human boundaries of gender or race, nonetheless chose twelve men to be His disciples, who then became the first elders in the church at Jerusalem. Jesus, who bowed to no boundaries but the ones set for Him by the Father, was bidden by the Father to choose twelve men. He could have chosen six men and six women, or any other combination, but He did not. Hence, we follow this biblical model.

Furthermore, the biblical pattern which calls for elders to be the husband of one wife has roots that the apostle Paul traced back to the principles set out in creation (1 Corinthians 11:3). In addition, only a man can meet the character qualifications set out in 1 Timothy 3 and Titus 1, because only a man can be the "husband of one wife." Therefore, we believe that only men can serve as elders in a local church.

Question: How much responsibility does an elder's wife have?

Answer: The character qualifications listed for women whose husbands serve as leaders in the church appear in 1 Timothy 3:11. Paul speaks to "wives," which in the immediate context refers to deacons' wives, but in light of the whole chapter includes elders' wives as well. The character qualifications for wives of church leaders are as follows: they are to "be dignified, not malicious gossips, but temperate and faithful in all things."

Specifically, an elder's wife must be mature, keep her tongue from hurtful gossip, not be addicted to anything, and be faithful.

Question: What if an elder's wife exerts undue influence on him as an elder? How do you control an elder's wife in that instance?

Answer: This is a tough issue. Because a husband and wife are one flesh, an elder's wife has a unique responsibility in helping her husband find the mind of Christ. What may happen, however, is that her well-meaning advice can cloud her husband's mind. The wife of an elder must pray for husband and support him as he listens to the Lord. Then she should submit any counsel she may have first to the Lord before passing it on to her husband. By so doing, she will avoid influencing their husband in ungodly ways. As long as wives have this heart, they will wonderfully support their husbands as they shepherd and oversee the flock.

The key point of faith for the wife is to be set free from what people think about her and her husband. If she cares too greatly about what people think, then she will determine her answer to the issue at hand based on appearances and try to manipulate or influence her husband accordingly. She must trust her Lord and her husband enough to find God's best answer, not the one that will be best received by her friends or critics at church.

Question: From a slightly different angle, how does an elder keep from letting his strong-willed wife influence or even control his ministry?

Answer: This can be a severe problem. I know at least one man who resigned from an elder team largely because of his wife's undue influence on him. Confidential issues are exactly that. Far too often a person from the Body has gone to the elders with a confidential issue, only to have that issue spread around the church by an elder's wife who couldn't hold her tongue.

Above all, an elder must listen first to his Lord, then to his wife, and then to others who are close to him. It is natural, given the one-flesh relationship, that an elder will talk about certain issues at home with his wife. He may ask her opinion, and that opinion may be both wise and valuable. But he must keep one thing very clear in his mind: his wife's voice is one input, his Lord's voice is the deciding factor.

It is incumbent on an elder's brothers around the elder table to call a man into account if he is being controlled by his wife. This is one of the toughest problems an elder team faces, and must be handled with a great deal of delicacy and prayer. Since there is the residue of Adam in every elder, this problem will rear its head in some form or another in every elder's life, and he must choose to attune his ear first to his Lord's voice above all others.

Question: How do you train new elders?

Answer: Elders must be committed to consistently disciple younger men in the Scriptures. This is done by teaching them how to study and teach the Scriptures and by walking alongside them for a year or two. Over time, this process will continually develop new elders.

Another excellent proving ground for elders is to serve for a year or more as an apprentice elder, or "elder advisors." These men are invited to all the elder meetings. They are asked for their input, and they are asked to pray and reach conclusions just as other elders, but they do not officially make decisions. As time goes by, it becomes clear whether these men should be considered for eldership or not.

Question: What happens when you just can't reach unanimity?

Answer: You do nothing! The temptation when one or two men are holding out is to coerce them into making a decision just to get unanimity. But coercion or any other form of subtle pressure is strictly forbidden if true Spirit-led unanimity is to be achieved.

If you can't reach unanimity, then you have not yet clearly understood the mind of Christ, or His timing requires a delay. When this happens, three things are called for: keep praying, do more homework (study of the word, pray, thinking, consulting), and be patient! (For a more complete description of what to do in these circumstances, see chapter 8.)

Question: Can a unanimous decision of the elders be wrong?

Answer: This is the toughest of all questions to answer, because it is fraught with peril on every side. We must caution against assuming we have the wisdom to assess what is "right" or "wrong" on any decision that our Lord may truly author. His ways are not our ways, and a decision with which we are not comfortable is nonetheless His inscrutable plan for us or for our church.

If everything has been done in accordance with the Scripture, a unanimous decision of the elders cannot be wrong. Pragmatically speaking, however, a unanimous decision of the elders may be fraught with improprieties that render it incorrect. If a decision is made and it quickly becomes apparent that it is wrong, then some questions need to be asked.

First, are all the elders qualified according to the qualifications of 1 Timothy 3 and Titus 1? If so, then did each elder wrestle with the issue by praying and by listening, or was one of the elders coerced in his decision? If every man is clear that he prayed and sought the mind of Christ, and that there was no coercion or subtle outside influence underpinning the decision, then a third question should be asked: was the decision arrived at too hastily? If each man agrees that a reasonable time period went by to ensure that the Lord had ample opportunity to lead the elders, then it would seem that the decision was not "wrongly arrived at."

In the end, if each man has a strong sense that the Lord authored the decision, then all involved must trust God that He was sovereignly working through the elders to reflect His mind—

even if it seems like a colossal mistake. We can take comfort from the fact that one Friday afternoon in Jerusalem, it seemed like God had made the greatest mistake in history. But by Sunday morning that "mistake" became His greatest victory of all time! Amen and amen!

APPENDIX II

Elder Training: Key Concepts

The following is an actual document in use at one church as a training guide for what elders need to know to serve faithfully:

A. The New Covenant

One of the current pastors or elders should teach the group the text of 2 Corinthians 3:6–9 in an inductive format with lots of application and insight into the life of Paul personally. The book Authentic Christianity by Ray Stedman can be used as reference for the person doing the teaching, but there needs to be lots of time for question and interaction. Another helpful text is The New

Covenant in the Old Testament by Dave Roper which should be required reading as part of this subject.

B. Expository Teaching/The New Covenant

A clear presentation should be made of what expository teaching is, including some general guidelines on how to exposit God's Word. This does not require getting into original languages, but does necessitate good explanation of some of the helps to expositing the Scriptures. This could include how to use Bible study tools like the following:

> *Waltke's Theological Wordbook of the Old Testament*
> *The Treasury of Scripture Knowledge*
> *Robertson's Word Pictures in the New Testament,*
> *Vine's Expository Dictionary of Bible Words,*
> Bible dictionaries and encyclopedias, concordances,
>   selected expository commentaries such as F. F. Bruce
>   and G. Campbell Morgan, etc.

Each person should be assigned a text of Scripture that features the New Covenant and be asked to teach it to the rest of the group with a frank but gracious critique following. Some of the passages of Scripture that might be considered would be: Hebrews 4:9–13, Galatians 2:20, Jeremiah 31:32–35, and John 15:1–8.

C. Church Government and Servant Leadership

A thorough discussion on this subject should be made, perhaps teaching from Mark 10:35–45. Additionally, a practical discussion should take place on how unanimity is obtained, and its basis in Scripture (such as Acts 15—the Jerusalem Council decision.)

D. Finances

A practical discussion needs to occur concerning how the Lord leads in the area of finances. Subjects to be considered:

1. giving without coercion
2. keeping records after the fact without predicting the future
3. procedures for check signing
4. procedures if there aren't sufficient funds—who gets paid first
5. procedures on special gifts from the Body to individuals
6. reporting to the Body
7. procedures for evaluating salaries of employees
8. procedures for how staff spends money and how their expenses are evaluated
9. how capital expenditures are determined
10. the issue of corporate debt
11. how to help pastors purchase their own homes
12. how intern finances are handled

E. Evaluation of Elders/Pastors

Utilizing the Timothy and Titus passages, a thorough exposition and study should review the qualifications for elders and how those are utilized in practice. Also required is a discussion of periodic evaluation by all pastors and elders of one another. This discussion should include the procedures and safeguards.

F.   Church Discipline

A careful examination of Matthew 18 and how the Body is encouraged to function in this area should be conducted. Utilizing PBC's experience with Richard Seafair should be helpful.

G.   Shepherding

A thorough discussion and interaction on the subject of shepherding using such passages as John 21:15–23, and 1 Peter 5:1–11 is necessary.

H.   Discipleship

A thorough discussion of discipleship from the text of Acts 20:17–38. Dave Roper's materials on discipleship are helpful.

I.   Weddings

One of the pastors should go through the procedures for premarital counseling that he uses plus how to use a Taylor-Johnson Temperament Analysis Test, and what books and/or taped or recorded messages he gives to the couple to read. He should give a complete explanation of the passages that are used during premarital counseling (Genesis 2:18–25 and Ephesians 5:21–33). Also, examples of various kinds of ceremonies, which have been commonly used, would be very helpful for an elder when he is doing a marriage ceremony.

J. Funerals

A discussion of memorial services, funerals, and what to do at the graveside should be taught along with all the various passages of Scripture that can be used. Also, how best to present the gospel at a funeral and counsel the bereaved and close relatives is important.

K. Counseling in General

A discussion should be carried out on the basis of biblical counseling. Material by Dr. John Edrington (a four-part series on preparing to counsel) is excellent. It is not necessary to do an in-depth treatment of counseling, because elders by their very qualifications are wise and godly men who are already qualified for much of their counseling. But it is a good idea to have available a list of books on counseling, such as Henry Brandt's *Heart of the Problem* for reference. Also, a list of competent professional counselors in the area for referrals should be supplied.

L. Hospital Visitation

A discussion similar to item "K" should take place on this subject.

M. Spiritual Gifts

This is a critical subject for elders to thoroughly understand, so they can help the Body discern their spiritual gifts and put them to work. Passages to examine are Ephesians 4, 1 Peter 4, 1 Corinthians 12, and Romans 12.

N. Body Life

Elders and pastors set the atmosphere for Body Life in a local church. An understanding of how the members of the Body of Jesus Christ care for one another, bear each other's burdens, and minister one on one or in groups, is therefore vital. Ray Stedman's book, *Body Life,* is well worth reading.

O. Spiritual Warfare

The apostle Paul says, "We wrestle not against flesh and blood, but against principalities and powers . . . against spiritual forces of wickedness" (Ephesians 6:12). Elders must understand what we are to do and then help the Body in their struggle. Understanding Satan and his schemes (drawn from Old and New Testament Scriptures), plus a thorough examination of Ephesians 6:10–20, is necessary.

P. The Christian Home

In our culture, this subject needs special emphasis. Elders need to be grounded in the following:

being a loving husband	Ephesians 5:18–33
being a father and a priest	Ephesians 6:1–4
being a teacher and example	Deuteronomy 6:4–9
being a wise parent and teaching wisdom	Proverbs 2:1–22
being a moral mentor and imparting	
truth about sex	Proverbs 5:1–23
truth about relationships	Proverbs 7:1–27
truth about living life wisely	Proverbs 1 – 9

About the Authors

Paul Winslow is associate pastor at Valley Bible Church in Veradale, Washington, outside Spokane, where he has served since 1991. Prior to that he worked as associate pastor at Peninsula Bible Church in Palo Alto, California, from 1972 to 1991.

Paul has a degree in mechanical engineering from the University of Washington. He and his wife Karen have been married since 1962. They have three children and six grandchildren.

Dorman Followwill is a management consultant and a 1985 graduate of Stanford University. He married his wife Blythe upon his graduation, and served for a time as the university pastor at Peninsula Bible Church. Dorman has been an associate pastor at several other churches. He and Blythe have five children.

If you would like to contact the authors by e-mail, you may do so at phwinslow@juno.com.

If *Christ in Church Leadership* challenged your soul, you'll want to read Ray Stedman's book *Body Life*. Mr. Stedman was a pastor at Peninsula Bible Church in Palo Alto, California, for more than 40 years, and an accomplished author. He was also a friend, companion, and coworker with Paul Winslow as they served together at PBC.

Body Life provides a wonderful complement to *Christ in Church Leadership* as it focuses attention on the real meaning and mission Christ intended for His church. Ask us about *Body Life* and other titles by Ray Stedman by contacting us here at Discovery House Publishers. You may write us at:

Discovery House Publishers
P. O. Box 3566
Grand Rapids, MI 49501 USA

You may also call us at 1-800-653-8333. Or visit us on the Internet at http://www.dhp.org/ or send e-mail to books@dhp.org.

Note to the Reader

The publisher invites you to share your response to the message of this book by writing Discovery House Publishers, P. O. Box 3566, Grand Rapids, MI 49501, USA or by calling 1-800-653-8333. For information about other Discovery House publications, contact us at the same address and phone number. Find us on the Internet at http://www.dhp.org/ or send e-mail to books@dhp.org.